Culture and the Media

Key Concerns in Media Studies

Series editor: Andrew Crisell

Within the context of today's global, digital environment, *Key Concerns in Media Studies* addresses themes and concepts that are integral to the study of media. Concisely written by leading academics, the books consider the historical development of these themes and the theories that underpin them, and assess their overall significance, using up-to-date examples and case studies throughout. By giving a clear overview of each topic, the series provides an ideal starting point for all students of modern media.

Published

Paul Bowman   *Culture and the Media*

Andrew Crisell   *Liveness and Recording in the Media*

Tim Dwyer   *Legal and Ethical Issues in the Media*

Gerard Goggin   *New Technologies and the Media*

Shaun Moores   *Media, Place and Mobility*

Forthcoming

Gerard Goggin and Kathleen Ellis   *Disability and the Media*

David Hendy   *Public Service Broadcasting*

Niall Richardson and Sadie   *Wearing Gender and the Media*

Culture and the Media

Paul Bowman

Cardiff University, UK

palgrave
macmillan

First published 2012 by
PALGRAVE MACMILLAN

Palgrave Macmillan in the UK is an imprint of Macmillan Publishers Limited, registered in England, company number 785998, of Houndmills, Basingstoke, Hampshire RG21 6XS.

Palgrave Macmillan in the US is a division of St Martin's Press LLC, 175 Fifth Avenue, New York, NY 10010.

Palgrave Macmillan is the global academic imprint of the above companies and has companies and representatives throughout the world.

Palgrave® and Macmillan® are registered trademarks in the United States, the United Kingdom, Europe and other countries.

ISBN 978–0–230–27712–0

This book is printed on paper suitable for recycling and made from fully managed and sustained forest sources. Logging, pulping and manufacturing processes are expected to conform to the environmental regulations of the country of origin.

A catalogue record for this book is available from the British Library.

A catalog record for this book is available from the Library of Congress.

10   9   8   7   6   5   4   3   2   1
21   20   19   18   17   16   15   14   13   12

Printed and bound in Great Britain by
CPI Antony Rowe, Chippenham and Eastbourne

Contents

Introduction

Textbooks can be boring. Introductions can be patronising. The book that you are now reading – or previewing, leafing through, or otherwise thinking about reading – is neither simply an introduction nor simply a textbook. Whether or not you want to read one, I certainly didn't want to write one. So I did not. Nevertheless, I have tried to write a book that *could* be read by people who have never read anything of media or cultural studies – a book that *could* be a first encounter with these two fields, but a book that does not try to cover everything in some supposedly systematic, encyclopaedic way. This book is not encyclopaedic. Instead, it explores some important aspects of the relationships between what we term 'media' and 'culture'.

This book explores aspects of media and culture in different ways. Chapter 1 begins by directly posing the question of the relationship between media and culture. This is a complicated matter. First of all it is a question of definition: how do you define either of these two things? Secondly, it is a matter of demarcating them: where does culture or the media 'stop'? Thirdly, it opens out onto philosophical, theoretical or ontological problems: in what sense, where and how, could these things be said to exist?

To explore, illustrate and amplify some of the grounds that the answers to these questions cover, the chapter discusses them with references to some classic media-shocks and scandals – specifically the moral panics around the emergence of the punk rock phenomenon on British TV and in the British press in the UK in the 1970s. Other examples could be given – and the open invitation that I hope readers will accept is to treat the examples that I analyse in these pages not as definitive or comprehensive examples, but rather as interesting and thought-provoking cases, which make no claim to being unique. Hopefully the arguments and insights proposed about them will have a wider relevance and currency. Of course, as with all reading and all interpretation, one must join the dots oneself. Sometimes one must first draw the dots by oneself too, and then join them. The point is, reading and interpretation are processes of active engagement and construction, rather than passive reception.

Chapter 2 is organised by the idea of interconnectedness. By way of examples from popular culture (mainly film), like Chapter 1, Chapter 2 explores some of the key ways in which various forms of cultural and media interconnectedness have been theorised and analysed in media and cultural studies – or, rather, in the pre-history of these fields. For, there were thinkers asking questions about culture and the media long before we had the named academic disciplines of media studies and cultural studies; and the chapter pulls in quite a few perspectives that are not always deemed 'proper' cultural studies or 'proper' media studies. In doing so, you might say, the chapter does a kind of violence to the idea of a 'proper' way to approach things.

Chapter 3 takes the idea of doing violence to 'the proper' even further. It is organised by the idea of the constructedness of culture and of media texts and processes. Culture is always constructed. Media texts, perspectives and positions are always selective, hierarchical and ultimately therefore, censoring. Arguably then, different types of 'violence' are integral to both culture and to media. So the chapter explores some of these: from the 'violence' of editing and (mis)representation, to the violence of media representations (of violence), and the violence of politics and policing. But it circles around and points to some of the ways in which the inevitability of construction – cultural, political, argumentative and media construction – is also a chance and a source of hope. The question is one of *who* constructs and represents things. This is the crucial political, cultural and media question. Who constructs? Who represents? With what effects and what consequences?

No book can hope to answer things like this comprehensively or encyclopaedically. What this book hopes to do is to draw attention to some of the complex and ingrained problems related to the fact of culture as constructed and mediated. Chapter 4 delves deeper into some of these effects, by reading a few media texts – textual examples that have a wider significance in terms of what they can teach us about how culture and the media interact in productive ways.

And after all this, where will we have got to? Where will we have been? Where will we have arrived? Where will we have travelled? On a surface reading – judging a book by its cover or by its table of contents – not very far. And this is indeed true: this book does not cover all or even many realms and registers or possible forms of the relationship between culture and the media. But, really, how could it? I would propose that any single book which claims to do so is likely to be either boring or patronising, or both. Rather, I would like to hope instead that in delving into the relations – just some of the relations – between culture and the media, in this way, we will nevertheless have gained a significant amount of insight, which can be taken and applied in further contexts and to further questions of culture and the media.

1 Culture Is (Not) the Media

'Culture and the media?' What and the what?

The title of this book, *Culture and the Media*, implies that we know what the terms 'culture' and 'the media' mean. It also implies that they are different things – that 'culture' is distinct from the media, and that 'the media' is distinct from culture. So, the title suggests that culture and the media are distinct but that there is some kind of relationship between them. Yet is this the case? Things are not so simple. Culture has many possible definitions, and none are universally accepted. A term like 'the media' is deceptive: it implies that 'the media' is a fixed group of things, a closed club of definite members or a short list made up of a few familiar figures. But who are the familiar figures? What do we include in a list of the media? Radio, TV and film are the usual suspects. These technologies were surely the key players of the media in the 20th Century. Before that, national presses were prime movers, with national newspapers being at the cutting edge of 'the media'. Before that, and at the same time, running alongside, other institutions mediated, disseminated and publicised information – books, journals and records, although we don't normally include such things in a list of media. And, more recently, of course, following the advent of the World Wide Web in the late 20th Century, all manner of new technologies are not only proliferating, but also blurring the possible distinctions between the media and culture.

The reverse is also true. For, historically, national presses, regional and national newspapers, not to mention radio, TV, film and other practices, have long played crucial roles in nation-building. They have, in other words, worked culturally. That is, the media have worked to build senses of shared interest, shared position, shared perspective and collective identity among members of a geographical territory (a country). And this is surely a key dimension of producing a sense of shared *culture*.

So, 'the media' appears to be anything but distinct from 'culture'. Indeed, because the media are so important for disseminating ideas, setting out various positions and introducing certain debates and perspectives into untold numbers of contexts and daily lives, the national press should also be seen to be involved in processes that would have to be called not only cultural but also *political*. This suggests that aspects of both culture and politics are inextricably entwined with the media. As such, any list of the contents of the supposedly separate categories of 'culture', 'the media' and 'politics' can seem like a kind of double or triple counting of the same thing – a bit like saying 'this club has three members: me, myself and I'.

So, ultimately, given their evidently interlocking relationships, how can the three things already mentioned here (culture, politics and the media), as well as related entities like society or the economy, be understood as separate, discrete or self-contained? And if they cannot be regarded as separate or properly distinct, then on what grounds can we justifiably separate them out, as if they really are separate things? In other words: if culture and the media cannot really be separated out, then are such familiar terms as 'culture' and 'the media' of any academic or analytic use? Are they real terms for designating real things? Or are they sloppy and imprecise terms? We certainly use the terms in everyday life, but are they the best terms? Are they the most precise? Are they even 'correct'?

Familiar impossible terms

At this point, you might expect a book with the title *Culture and the Media* to dive into a long series of definitions and specifications, clarifying what we 'therefore' ought to understand by the terms 'culture' and 'media'. This would be a reasonable direction to take. However, instead of doing this, I would like us to start from different premises, make different assumptions and proceed according to a different style altogether. Specifically – and somewhat surprisingly, perhaps, given this book's title – I would like to propose, before we rush into things, that there may be no such things as 'culture' and 'the media'. They may not exist, as such. They may not exist in a relationship. They may not exist at all.

I am not saying that they definitely don't exist. I am saying instead that they might not be quite what we think they are. They might not be the obvious and immediately intelligible things that we assume. They might not be two distinct things. We might need some better terms. Words like 'culture' and categories like 'the media' might not really be well-formed. Despite their familiarity, they might not really refer to real things – in much the same way as words like 'germs' or 'Martians' do not really refer to real things. So, what I want to do is to *defamiliarise* the terms, to urge caution and to enquire into what we might actually be referring to when we evoke 'culture' or 'the media'.

One of the basic operations of the academic approach called *deconstruction* is to put familiar terms into question. In this case, let's notice, *we think we already know* what 'media' and 'culture' mean. But before rushing headlong into discussing them, we should take some time to make sure we are clear on exactly what we are discussing. This is an important stage of any academic study: to clearly specify and define the terms. However, in deconstruction, the effort to clarify what a term means, or how to distinguish it from other terms, generally leads to a sense that we cannot easily or reliably distinguish one thing from another. Some people say that therefore deconstruction is not helpful for media or cultural study. However, what deconstruction does is draw our attention to the fact that whenever we *make* a definition or *draw* a distinction, this act is not 'natural' or 'inevitable', and is always a decision – one that it is best to make deliberately and consciously, rather than 'automatically' or without thinking about why we make the distinctions and definitions that we do.

According to Raymond Williams, one of the earliest pioneers and enduringly influential figures of cultural studies, 'Culture is one of the two or three most complicated words in the English language' (Williams 1976: 76). He continues: 'This is so partly because of its intricate historical development, in several European languages, but mainly because it has now come to be used for important concepts in several distinct intellectual disciplines and in several distinct and incompatible systems of thought' (1976: 76–77). In other words, it has a complicated history – in fact, several simultaneously complicated histories – sometimes overlapping, sometimes existing in different contexts. So whenever we use the term 'culture', although we may think that we all understand it in the same way and agree on what it means, we may all in fact mean very different things by it. Moreover, we might not even notice that there is a disagreement about meaning, because the term is so completely familiar to us all. We might not even enquire any further into what 'culture' may mean.

The philosopher G. W. F. Hegel puts it this way: 'What is "familiarly known" is not properly known, just for the reason that it is "familiar"' (Hegel 1910/2005: 92). In other words, just because we are familiar with a thing, a phenomenon, a term or a notion, this does not mean that we 'know' it. The names and terms for many things are merely 'fixed points', Hegel argues, and we use them, discuss them and debate them, but what we have all too often done, suggests Hegel, is to have 'uncritically presupposed' that we understand the things we are talking about. We *think* that we know them *because* they are familiar, but all we are doing really is bandying about terms ('fixed points') as if we know them. This kind of 'process of knowing', says Hegel, 'flits between these secure points, and in consequence goes on merely along the surface'. Accordingly, this kind of 'knowing' is not thorough or precise *knowing*, but is rather, according to Hegel, 'the commonest form of self-deception' (Hegel 1910/2005: 92).[1]

The point is this: there are lots of terms in the world, lots of words in our language, terms that we bandy about every day, terms that we think we understand because they are familiar. But they don't necessarily even exist. Yet we use them as if they do. Or they may exist, but we don't necessarily understand them or know exactly what we are talking about even when talking about them. Think of terms like 'God', for example, or 'sin', or 'Father Christmas', 'Martians', 'gremlins', 'luck', 'unicorns', 'peace' or 'eternity'. These are all very familiar ideas to many people in the world. But do they *exist*? Are they *real*? Or rather, in what sense could they be said to exist? In what sense, other than familiarity, do we *know* them?

Discourse

All of these things (and many more that we could add) exist as part of a *discourse*. 'God' exists as part of theological discourses. Some of the discourses about God also include notions like sin and redemption; some also include peace and eternity. Martians certainly exist as part of science fiction discourses. Gremlins, luck and unicorns exist as part of a wide spectrum of discourses: stories, myths, legends, narratives, fantasies, beliefs, books, toys, playthings, pictures and all sorts of other products and practices. But none of these things necessarily exist *as such*, 'out there', in the world. They do not exist in the same way that we could say we know trees exist or clouds. There may be no Father Christmas out there, whether living at the North Pole or in Greenland or Lapland or anywhere else. There may be no God 'out there' somewhere, perhaps sitting on a cloud in a place called 'Heaven'. But there definitely are discourses about God. Father Christmas and God definitely exist within discourses. We are familiar with the terms. There are conversations about them. There are believers and dissenters. Moreover, and more importantly, there are institutions and conventions. There are traditions and breaks with tradition. There are conventions, conflicts and consequences related to these traditions and institutions. People do things that are informed by, or even organised by these terms. This is what is meant by *discourse*. There is definitely a real discourse, or set of discourses, about God. These have real consequences in the real world. This is so even if God does not exist in the way many people want 'him' or 'her' or 'it' to exist.

In other words, we can see that there are discourses about many things – things which may or may not exist in the ways we normally mean when we say 'such-and-such exists'. Discourses about things exist. The things about which there are discourses may not exist: God, Heaven, Afterlife, Father Christmas, Freedom, Justice, Equality, Culture...These may not exist. But we know that discourses about these things exist, and we can see what they are and what they do. Discourses are conversations – spoken or written – and they often have effects. One can see that discourses about God have had all sorts of effects: believers, disciples, institutions; sacred books, sacred figures, places of worship and other kinds of institutions; powerful figures, disputes, disagreements, outcasts, exiles, upheavals; acts, actions, legislations, battles, invasions, wars, atrocities, acts of kindness, generosity, selfishness, selflessness, sacrifice, persecution, murder, suicide, sacrifice, love, cynicism...

But this is not a book about God. God here is just an example of something that may or may not exist but that certainly really exists in real *discourses* in the real world. The point of using the term 'God' as an example is because God is such a familiar term, so central to so many aspects of worldly life, beliefs and institutions, and yet so *unknown*. Again, all I want to assert here is that we should perhaps hesitate before assuming that just because a term is familiar, it refers to something real, something that we know or understand.

'Culture' and 'the media' are equally familiar terms. But perhaps they do not exist in quite the way that these clear and distinct terms suggest. Perhaps saying 'culture' is a bit like saying 'Heaven': we can discuss and speculate about it. But is there such a thing? Or more tangibly: perhaps using the word 'culture' is a bit like using a word like 'weather'. Perhaps saying 'the media' is a bit like saying the word 'electricity'. A word like 'weather' tells us everything and yet nothing. There is always weather, but it's often not noticeable. It is most noticeable when there are extreme weather events. Weather is always a *process*. It is sometimes an *event*. It is produced by differential forces of heating and cooling of different materials with different effects. It is not really a 'thing'. It is something that *happens*. It is something that is always going on, more or less noticeable or noticed. The same goes for electricity. Knowing that there is power, that there is an electrical power supply, tells us nothing specific. It tells us nothing about what forms it takes, what it may be used for, what is or isn't being done with it or how it relates – if at all – to the weather.

The analogies I am playing around with here may strike you as interesting and thought-provoking, or you may find them confusing, irritating or annoying. Obviously, I hope that the former is the case. However, whether they work or not, my aim is merely to suggest that these familiar terms may not be anything like straightforward. This is so even though they are familiar.

A quick dip into the range of arguments about what culture and the media are and what they do reveals just how complex and disputed the terrain that we are now entering is. The terms 'culture' and 'media' have long histories and have had lots of effects. People use the terms and the notions in all sorts of different ways. People make different assumptions about the *ways* that they exist, *how* they exist and *where* they exist. There are lots of discourses and arguments about 'culture'. Lots of people have expended lots of energy pointing to different things and grading them as good or bad 'culture', good or bad 'media', superior or inferior things or processes. These are discourses that have raged for a very long time. However, they are particularly prominent when there are what we might term *extreme media events*.

The extremities of culture

Perhaps one of the first notable examples of an extreme media event is encapsulated in the discourse around the 1976 and 1977 pop songs 'Anarchy in the UK' (1976) and 'God Save the Queen' (1977). The performers were The Sex Pistols, who were at the time the most famous or infamous of the newly emerging phenomenon of punk rock in Britain.

The earlier song, 'Anarchy in the UK', voices the sentiment that anarchy 'is coming', and this was delivered by The Sex Pistols in a way that was either *calculated* to shock a perceived conservative establishment, or the mainstream in the UK, or that actually *reflected* the emergence of an extremely angry, belligerent, anti-establishment and potentially violent and scary element within British youth. Either way, the band *performed* anger, *enacted* the gestures of rebellion and youth insurrection. The vocals were more shouted than sung, and the harsh sound of the rock chords was unusual in mainstream music at the time. The TV and radio airplay given to The Sex Pistols made them the first punk rock band to become prominent in the UK. The theatrically bedraggled appearance and what was to some the almost incomprehensibly gratuitous aggressiveness of the performance of the band and their fans appeared to confirm not only the band's truculence but also the potential danger that they represented.

The perceived hostility to British society and – perhaps most of all – the apparent rejection of all deference to the status quo and to the hierarchies of British society evinced by The Sex Pistols and punk rock more widely generated a lot of media interest. It activated – or reactivated – a debate about British culture, values, acceptability, expectations, decency, behaviour, youth, tradition, crime, degeneracy and danger, a debate that was sociologically significant and that remains philosophically fascinating. What took place was in fact what sociologists came to call a 'moral panic' – a media-led panic about the perceived dangerous and damaging effects of the punk rock phenomenon on the 'fabric' of British society. This moral panic took place in the form of scandalised newspaper headlines and febrile radio and TV discussions about the likely degeneration of British society into anarchy because of the dissemination of such images, sounds and words among impressionable youth.

All of this was compounded and sharpened in the subsequent 1977 Sex Pistols single 'God Save the Queen'. If there had been any doubt that The Sex Pistols were keen to attack the most sacred aspects of British nationalistic pride and tradition, 'God Save the Queen' clarified matters. The song was released to coincide with the British Queen's Silver Jubilee celebrations, and because of its relentlessly irreverent critique of the popular British institution of the Monarchy (its lyrics include lines such as the opening salvo of 'God save the Queen, the fascist regime', a concisely offensive sentiment to which more and more slurs are quickly added, including *ad hominem* innuendoes like 'God save the Queen, 'cos tourists are money, and our figurehead is not what she seems'), the song was banned from BBC radio airplay and yet reached Number 1 in the charts. Perhaps it reached number one *because* it was banned.[2]

There are many similar cases of the emergence of a putatively shocking, unusual or culturally problematic text, whether that be a work of literature or film, a pop song or computer game; many of these share the same features and experience the same sorts of reception as these 1970s Sex Pistols singles: they are widely reviled, frowned upon or banned, yet nevertheless become very popular and successful.

It is significant that so many supposedly 'shocking' texts activate and reactivate generalised debates about the terrible state of culture and society. In reaction to supposedly shocking spectacles like the Sex Pistols' songs, society quickly becomes represented as being 'in crisis'. In fact, time and again there is a regular coincidence of this or that 'shocking' text precipitating scandalised debate and mass moralising about culture and society being in 'crisis'. And what we can see from all of these is that judgements about the awfulness or badness of *this thing* reciprocally imply a judgement about the greatness or goodness of *that other thing*. In other words, value judgements about specific things imply wider understandings of what is to be valued and what 'the good' culture 'is'. In short, 'folk devils' are held up as the counterpoints to define the saints and angels of the good. A 'moral panic' also works as a rallying call to reassert what the good is or would ideally be like.

Moral panics occur regularly. Typically an identity, group, product, process or practice is singled out and declared to be something that threatens the very fabric of society – something that threatens to lead society into a collapse, through a crumbling of morality. Examples include rock 'n' roll, punk rock, drugs, alcohol, religious cults, television, 'video nasties', pornography, immigration, new types of technology or media such as the World Wide Web or specific aspects of it, computer games and so on. Examples can be added to this list. These often seem to share the features and characteristics of a media-led reaction to an increasingly scapegoated phenomenon, which is blamed for perceived moral and social problems.

Needless to say, the media are prime movers here, and in two senses: the media both publicises the crisis and is blamed for introducing the crisis in the first place. So a moral panic typically involves a febrile debate about what the ideal good media would be. Here, then, the media are regarded as supplements to and in the service (or abuse) of culture, without being regarded as a proper part of 'the' culture – whatever 'culture' is supposed to be. So, what is culture supposed to be?

(Un)Popular culture

In the face of the question of defining culture, there has been a variety of answers. For instance, 'culture' is sometimes regarded as something that 'cultured' people have. This position takes a characteristic part in what has come to be known as the 'high culture versus low culture' debate. Traditionally, the privilege of understanding what is 'best' has been given to the culture of the upper classes, and to their taste and values. The high class has the high culture. In this, the degree to which and the way in which you are 'cultured' is determined by your social class.

Alternatively, culture has been approached as if it is something that other people have – while 'we' are simply individuals. So, the others have one culture, while 'we' are different and unique individuals. In one sense, this understanding makes 'culture' the name of the dividing line along which 'others' are made to seem to be noticeably different from 'us'. In a second sense, this understanding implies that these others are 'all the same', while 'we' are all individuals. Ultimately, therefore, this is an irreducibly racist view: it reduces all others to a group identity, it says 'they are all the same', while it proposes that 'we' are unique, named, independent individuals. So, the others are made to seem like a swarm, a horde, a hive, or, of course, *a tribe*, while we are superior free consciousness.

The reciprocal or obverse formulation of this understanding is one which regards culture as something that 'we' have, that they don't: that is, the thing or things which make us different from and superior to 'them'. The other culture is *uncultured*, while we are *cultured*. This is a variation on the 'high versus low culture' debate, but it can be organised along regional, class, race, gender, employment, language, sub-cultural or other lines. It is infinitely supple and flexible. It is based on the production or invention of a differential – a point of difference that is asserted in discourse. And it shows that any binary differential that is produced in discourse is never going to be free from value judgements and hierarchy. The specification of 'us' versus 'them' is never going to be a harmonious balance of opposites, like the Buddhist Yin-Yang symbol. It is rather going to represent the initiation of a hierarchy: *this* is better than or superior to *that*.

Barbarian, philistine and popular culture

Whatever 'culture' *is* – if it *is* a 'thing' at all – what is clear is that the term is used in various discourses to organise, hierarchise, grade and value. We could argue, then, that there is always a political dimension to the use (and abuse) of the term 'culture': it always seems to involve putting groups and practices 'in their place', through the judgement of what is superior and what is inferior, what is to be valued and what is to be spurned. So, we could ask some preliminary questions: is 'culture' related to what is valued? Where do our values come from? Where do our tastes come from? What do different values and tastes 'mean'? Do they matter or make a difference? What are their implications? Who decides what is 'best'? Who decides what is 'right' and 'proper'? Who decides what is improper or wrong? What are the implications of different tastes and values? These are some of the first questions of cultural studies that we ought to explore.

'Culture' has had different meanings through time. From the mid-18th Century, it referred to the general process of intellectual and aesthetic development. From the early 19th Century, it referred to the particular way of life (the customs, traditions and values) of a people or group. From the end of the 19th Century, culture often referred to a specific set of artistic practices and products: art, literature, theatre, music and opera.

As Raymond Williams made clear, 'culture' still has many different meanings in different contexts. It has different meanings across different types of academic usage – varying across sociology, anthropology, political science and literary studies, as well as *within* these fields, according to which of many theoretical perspectives that is using the term, here or there, whether that be, for instance, Marxist, psychoanalytic, historicist, semiotic or any other of an ever-expanding range. Elsewhere, people talk about culture as if there are 'types': elite, high, bourgeois, dominant; mass, popular, working-class; national; sub-cultural; generational (youth, middle aged and old); local or regional (Geordie, Cockney); ethnic (black, Asian and white); sexual (gay, straight, 'bi'); the culture of a particular historical period (for example, 1960s culture); the culture(s) of this or that particular practice (pop culture, football and online communities); socio-economic (class); as well as mainstream, dominant, oppositional, emergent, residual and counterculture – to list but a few.

One interesting feature of many, particularly the early, approaches to culture is the extent to which 'popular culture' – or the culture of the masses, however conceived or named – was so often regarded as being inferior to the 'proper' culture of the elite. Moreover, popular culture was regarded not only as inferior but also as being a *problem*, and not only a problem but actually a field of degeneration, something culturally dangerous. People still view popular culture this way, of course. And these views regularly recur in debates and moralising about culture being in crisis in response to this or that shocking or scandalous text, such as 'Anarchy in the UK' or 'God Save the Queen' by The Sex Pistols in the 1970s.

One reason why I keep returning to these songs and the moral panic that blew up in response to them is because The Sex Pistols' chosen themes (anarchy, rejection and destruction of the current society, as well as its norms and values) resound so compellingly with the work of one of the first and most famous thinkers of culture (and anarchy), Matthew Arnold, who published the influential book *Culture and Anarchy* in 1869 (Arnold 2009). Within it, he forwarded a notion of culture as 'the best that has been thought and said in the world'. Moreover, culture is construed in this book as something to be 'attained' by intellectual effort. Culture is something to be *cultivated*. 'Popular culture', on the other hand, is anarchy – danger. How many times have we heard versions of this perspective since then? Certainly, quite a few.

Matthew Arnold sets out a perspective which regularly returns in different variations and slightly modified reiterations in debates about (popular) culture and, more recently, the media. Arnold's perspective has its own unique features, of course. For instance, Arnold regarded society as being made up of three essential social groups: first, a group he called Barbarians, by which he meant the aristocracy. For Arnold, the aristocracy are barbarians, because they are nothing other than the contemporary residues of the class who got to the top through violence and warfare. Their contemporary interests and conventions are telltale echoes of their martial past: hunting, horses, hounds, hierarchy....

Second, there are the philistines. These are the middle classes. They are philistines because they have no values other than money, as they rose to where they are through a dedication to trade. To focus so centrally in life on trade, commerce and the pursuit of money is something that has been widely reviled by philosophers, thinkers, artists and activists of many stripes throughout the ages. Nietzsche, for example, held bank managers and petty bureaucrats in the lowest contempt, precisely because they had no values other than those of their dedication to money. The revolutionary communist thinkers Karl Marx and Friedrich Engels, unsurprisingly, regarded the bourgeoisie, which arose as the dominant class through the spread of capitalism in the wake of the Industrial Revolution, as a destructive or levelling force, which would spread across the surface of the globe and remake the world in its own image. The postmodernist thinker Jean Baudrillard perhaps sums up the philosophical problems with the philistines or the bourgeoisie (the primary ministers of capitalism) when he proposed that 'the pursuit of objects is without an object': in other words, empty, endless, unsatisfying, *unsatisfiable* and without any purpose other than itself.

It has perhaps only been the theorists, philosophers and champions of free market capitalism who have wholeheartedly approved of Arnold's philistine class. However, some may argue that popular cultural champions of money, glitz, glamour and conspicuous consumption, such as celebrities, film stars and gangster rappers, are also to be regarded as ministers for the 'philosophically empty' pursuit of profit and money for its own sake. Significantly, though, Arnold, like many subsequent thinkers and theorists of 'the masses', was most worried about what he calls the populace – which is the working class. The barbarians and the philistines are predictable. The populace are not.

Arnold's critical categorisation of social classes may seem to put us all on a common footing: we are all equally 'uncultured'. But, for Arnold, it is nevertheless the aristocracy who, despite their barbaric past, are closer to something like an ideal of 'culture'. The populace, on the other hand, are like animals, and are to be feared. This conservative line of thought is common in English history. After all, it is always easiest and even understandably desirable to align oneself with the powers that be, especially if there is potential benefit from doing so. But, one might wonder why Arnold was so worried about the populace in this 1869 book? One answer is glaring: two years earlier, in 1876, working-class men in England and Wales had won the right to vote. In other words, Arnold's fear of 'cultural' degeneration is based on the fear of what might happen next, as uneducated plebs – who were regarded as *therefore* unqualified for the responsibility – had gained a hold in political decision-making. Ultimately, then, Arnold's fear of the masses is a fear of democracy. Like many thinkers, before and since, from Plato to the present, Arnold preferred the thought of a stable status quo, with familiar classes at the top, in the middle, and at the bottom, to the thought of the chaotic and unpredictable ongoing transformation which could happen if *just anyone* could vote for *just anyone* or *anything*, which is the hallmark of democracy – the rule of the *demos*, the majority, the people.

Like other notable thinkers, Arnold believed that the only way to ward off the catastrophe that would be caused by extending democracy to such groups as the great unwashed and unqualified would be to educate these groups properly. For Arnold, education could replace what the modern world had 'lost', namely, deference to and respect for authority. Education could cultivate a respect for culture (and eradicate dangerous popular culture). Education could avoid the 'anarchy' of social change. Education too, therefore, is to be regarded as a political force – a kind of power, to keep people valuing what they should value, doing what they should be doing, and, ideally, voting for who they should be voting for. Education becomes a kind of cultural–political force to manage the potentially disruptive force of not only popular culture but, more importantly, of democracy unleashed.

Arnold is not alone in holding this view. Classical and modern thinkers, thinkers on the left and thinkers on the right alike have often placed a stake in the potential power of education (or re-education) to combat the perceived threat of the collapse of society or the status quo because of the debasement caused by alien, foreign, new or low class 'cultural' influences. One of the most feared of potential pernicious influences, as we will see, has been and continues to be *the media*. The media, as we have come to think if it, does not feature all too prominently in the nightmares of Matthew Arnold, who, writing in the 1850s to 1870s, was more animated by the potential consequences involved in the giving of political power to the uneducated masses. But worries about the effects of the media on culture and society started to become more pronounced in later thinkers. Two of the most famous such commentators are T. S. Eliot, writing poetry and essays from the 1920s to the 1950s, and the literary critic F. R. Leavis, writing between the 1930s and 1970s.

Culture versus the media

Leavis and Eliot asked what culture is and how it is related to broader society. Their answer, essentially, was that there is high culture (elite culture, the arts) which *opposes* or is *opposed by* mass culture and popular culture, both of which are fuelled by and made worse by the media. As Eliot writes in *The Idea of a Christian Society* (1939):

The steady influence which operates silently in any mass society organised for profit, for the depression of standards of art and culture [is against the masses]. The increasing organization of advertisement and propaganda – or the influencing of masses of men by any means except through their intelligence – is all against them. The economic system is against them; the chaos of ideals and confusion of thought in our large-scale mass education is against them; and against them also is the disappearance of any class of people who recognize public and private responsibility of patronage of the best that is made and written.

(Eliot 1939: 40)

It is interesting to note that Eliot's 'conservative' position shares many coordinates in common with the Marxist position of the Frankfurt School intellectuals, Theodor Adorno and Max Horkheimer, who we will have reason to return to in due course. The media, they all concur, is driven by profit motives, by the imperatives and apparatuses of capitalism, and it is 'against' the masses. What is the solution? Again like the Marxists Adorno and Horkheimer, Eliot proposes the paradoxical solution that the best way to combat the degeneracy and corruption entailed by the massification of culture and society caused by such developments as urbanisation, the complex social machinery and architecture of modernity (mass housing, architecture and mass transport systems) and its media saturation is to insist on a traditional *elitism*. As Eliot wrote in *Notes towards the Definition of Culture*, 'it is an essential condition of the preservation of the quality of the culture of the minority, that it should continue to be a minority culture' (Eliot 1948: 107). The Marxists Adorno and Horkheimer felt much the same way – which just goes to show that elitism has many political faces.

But not all elitism is equal. Eliot, for instance, argues like many right-wing thinkers that culture boils down to identity. 'It will be their identity of belief and aspiration, their background of a common system of education and a common culture, which will enable them to influence and be influenced by each other, and collectively to form the conscious mind and conscience of the nation', he writes in *The Idea of a Christian Society* (1939). Even earlier, in 1934 – and in a way that is uncannily aligned with the time and ethos of the rise of Hitler and Nazism – Eliot had actually gone so far as to assert

The population should be homogenous; where two or more cultures exist in the same place they are likely either to be fiercely

self-conscious or both to become adulterate. What is still more important is unity of religious background; and reasons of race and religion
combine to make any large numbers of free-thinking Jews unde-
sirable. There must be a proper balance between urban and rural,
industrial and agricultural development. And a spirit of excessive
tolerance is to be deprecated.

(Eliot 1934: 20)

A lot could be said about Eliot's anti-Semitism. However, what deserves
mention above all here is the way it relates to a thinking of culture
as *identity* or *unity* and culture as *purity*. This equation is common in
approaches to culture. Fantasies of *purity* are often mixed with *nostalgia* –
as if things were better in some mythical past, when things were simpler
and purer, 'before' the others arrived or 'before' the pernicious influences from the outside, whether that be immigrants or American TV
shows on British screens, or whatever. For instance, at the same time as
Eliot was worrying about the corruption of culture that he perceived in
the productions of capitalism and all forms of cultural intermingling,
the famous literary critic F. R. Leavis was also to be found arguing about
English culture:

What we have lost is the organic community with the living culture it
embodied. Folk-songs, folk-dances, Cotswold cottages and handicraft
products are signs and expressions of something more: an art of life,
a way of living, ordered and patterned, involving social arts, codes of
intercourse and a responsive adjustment, growing out of immemo-
rial experience, to the natural environment and the rhythm of
the year.

(Leavis and Thompson 1933: 1)

For Leavis, and many who would follow him, the problem was 'mech-
anization', 'urbanization' and 'Americanization'. Another word for all
of this is *modernity*. The advent of modernity, with the proliferation of
industrialisation, massification, the rise of the metropolis, the group-
ing and atomisation of society (think of people living in skyscrapers or
tower blocks: squashed together in space yet absolutely separated from
each other in life – compartmentalised, atomised) produced anxiety
and nostalgia in thinkers of culture and society. Whether intention-
ally or accidentally echoing the great prophetic text of Karl Marx and
Friedrich Engels of a century before (*The Communist Manifesto*), in the
1930s F. R. Leavis wrote this:

The great agent of change, and, from our point of view, destruction, has been the machine – applied power. The machine has brought us many advantages, but it has destroyed the old ways of life, the old forms, and by reason of the continual rapid change it involves, prevented the growth of new. Moreover, the advantage it brings us in mass-production has turned out to involve standardization and levelling-down outside the realm of mere material goods. Those who in school are offered (perhaps) the beginnings of education in taste are exposed, out of school, to the competing exploitation of the cheapest emotional responses; films, newspapers, publicity in all its forms, commercially-created fiction – all offer satisfaction at the lowest level, and inculcate the choosing of the most immediate pleasures, got with the least effort . We cannot, as we might in a healthy state of culture, leave the citizen to be formed unconsciously by his environment; if anything like a worthy idea of satisfactory living is to be saved, he must be trained to discriminate and to resist.

(Leavis and Thompson 1933: 5)

Here we see 'culture' aligned with the past, with tradition, and with 'before' – before the invasion of the machines, among which the machines of the media are prime. The media is part of the mechanisation – and hence destruction – of culture (the past). The sole solution, the sole resistance, is to be found in education, in training people 'to discriminate and resist' the debasement of the world by industrialisation and media. Literature here is prime, because, 'if language tends to be debased ... instead of invigorated by contemporary use, then it is to literature alone, where its subtlest and finest use is preserved, that we can look with any hope of keeping in touch with our spiritual tradition – with the "picked experience of ages" ' (Leavis and Thompson 1933: 82).

The connections between Leavis and the earlier Marx as well as the subsequent radical thinkers who would come to be called the post-structuralists, such as Michel Foucault and Jacques Derrida, are uncanny. For, like Marx's forces of capitalism, Leavis's 'machine' has the same effects. As Leavis puts it, 'The machine has brought us many advantages, but it has destroyed the old ways of life, the old forms, and by reason of the continual rapid change it involves, prevented the growth of new'. For Marx and Engels a century earlier: 'All fixed, fast-frozen relations, with their train of ancient and venerable prejudices and opinions are swept away, all new-formed ones become antiquated before they can ossify. All that is solid melts into air, all that is sacred is profaned' (Marx and Engels 1967: 83).

However, for Marx, the ultimate consequence of the spread of capitalism was to be the spread of the exploitation of labour and hence the production of a universal class of workers who could and should rise up to seize the means of production in order to produce a communist future free from exploitation. But for Leavis the spread of modernity is regarded chiefly as the spread of cultural homogeneity and a debasement which starts and ends with the debasement of the building blocks of 'culture', in particular of 'language': 'if language tends to be debased ... instead of invigorated by contemporary use, then it is to literature alone, where its subtlest and finest use is preserved, that we can look with any hope of keeping in touch with our spiritual tradition'. One sees a similar sentiment in post-structuralist philosophers such as Foucault, Derrida and Kristeva, who perceived in literature the potentially emancipatory possibility of 'otherness' and 'difference' from the banal here and now of our everyday workaday world. Indeed, here we could oppose an idea of 'literary language' or 'cultured language' to 'media language'. Accordingly, culture and the media might become regarded as apparently opposed again.

The emancipatory potential of 'literature' is a proposition that cannot really be examined in any depth here. But thinkers of different sorts of ethical, political and philosophical stripes have seriously entertained one or another version of the belief that capital-a Art or capital-l Literature could 'save us' from the denuding or deleterious effects of mass media, mass marketing or simple stupidity.

In Leavis, it is clear that *literature* is an example of *culture* and is as such to be opposed to or distinguished from *media* or the *machine*. This can be seen, for instance, when he concedes that literary training alone 'is an inadequate response' to the onslaught of the profit-driven debasement of culture: 'Practical criticism of literature must be associated with training in awareness of the environment – advertising, the cinema, the press, architecture, and so on, for, clearly to the pervasive counter-influence of the environment the literary training of sensibility in school is an inadequate response' (Leavis 1943: 10). In other words, Leavis proposes the need for a kind of media and cultural studies education for students as a strategic response to the saturation of culture and society with retarding media images and inferior popular culture. But in such a 'Leavisite' media and cultural studies, one can be sure, the orientation would be one in which all types of text or phenomena other than traditional forms of Literature and Art would be compared unfavourably and found to be wanting. (Thankfully, this is not the direction that media and cultural studies took when they emerged throughout the 1960s and 1970s.)

Culture *as* media

Given the centrality of cultural forms such as literature in many defences of 'culture', and given that such so-called cultural forms are privileged over 'media' forms or newer technologies such as radio, film or TV, it seems pertinent to ask the following questions: in what way is literature *not* 'media'? By extension, in what way is 'culture' not 'mediated'?

The philosopher Jacques Derrida once focused on the question of the (supposed) borders between literature and philosophy. He questioned the existence or necessity of those borders for a number of reasons. For instance, both literature and philosophy are types of writing, he argues, and the key difference between them is that one imposes rules upon itself (academic philosophy, the *discipline* of philosophy), while the other operates in a different range of registers, styles and forms.[3] Moreover, along the way, Derrida notes this:

> Literature is a public institution of recent invention, with a comparatively short history, governed by all sorts of conventions connected to the evolution of law, which allows, in principle, anything to be said. Thus, what defines literature as such, within a certain European history, is profoundly connected with a revolution in law and politics: the principled authorization that anything can be said publicly.
> (Derrida 1996: 80)

Two things, at least, are important here. The first, for Derrida, is that literature becomes a socially recognisable institution as a result of other social institutions. The British legal process which culminated in the decision that *Lady Chatterley's Lover* by D. H. Lawrence was not to be regarded as pornography but rather as art is one example of the way in which the notion of 'literature' as a specific type or institution of writing has developed in some countries and contexts – but not in all: in some contexts, Salman Rushdie's book *The Satanic Verses*, for instance, is not regarded as an acceptable work of fictional literature, but rather as an unacceptable work of religious blasphemy.

Whether or not one is personally offended by a text is secondary to the matter of its legal status; the point being that the institution, the category, the convention and the very intelligibility of literature as literature is dependent on a very specific history. Literature as a social category, and specific forms of literature within it, emerged through struggles in history. In other words, as Derrida makes clear, it is not just that professional academic philosophers will write in one manner, while novelists could be said to have many more styles of writing open to them (including the option of being creative and constructing new styles). It is more importantly a matter of the historical struggles in law and politics through which a society comes to the situation where it allows that something called 'literature' can proceed in light of 'the principled authorisation that anything can be said publicly' within its pages. Were it not for such legal status, literature as a notion or a practice may not exist, or it may be – as it still is in many parts of the world – heavily censored and controlled. It is not a given. Nothing is a given. *Any* kind of social institution or practice is dependent on a complex history. *Everything is contingent.*

Moreover, in being *published*, literature is clearly a type of *public* speech. It relies on certain types of technological organisation, dissemination and circulation. To be regarded as 'fiction', this implies a certain type of reader, well-versed in a certain type of reading – someone who 'knows' that these words on these pages are 'not real' – so, someone who 'knows' that *Lady Chatterley's Lover* is 'not porn' and someone who 'knows' that the potentially religiously offensive scenes in *The Satanic Verses* are not simply the beliefs of the author. The 'proper' reader of modern novels 'knows' that the words contained within the pages of this or that novel are not really or necessarily or verifiably those of its author. Even the word 'I' in a novel cannot be read as being the voice of the author. The 'I' in literature is the voice of a character or the narrative voice of the narrator, who may or may not seem to be that of a character within the story or some version or persona of the author. In short, the ideal reader of literature is someone who recognises that literature is literature. Even so, just to be sure, most published books – and, even more prominently, products such as films on DVD, Blu-rays and downloads – carry a legal disclaimer which states that the views and opinions expressed herein are not those of the company. Just to be sure.

Misunderstandings can occur. Even the so-called father of Western Philosophy, Plato, argued that any type of art that created fictions should be excluded from the ideal republic. This is because fictions are still messages and forms of communication, and they can be disruptive and distracting – or, indeed, subversive. So, we may say, even literature – this supposedly 'timeless' institution of 'culture' – involves a type of messaging, a type of communication, and amounts, therefore, to functioning also as a type of media.

The disagreement of culture

Culture is essentially perhaps little more than an *argument*. For it is a term that is often bandied about, often part of passionate arguments and always seems to refer to something that is never quite there and never quite that. The essence of culture is never fully or properly specifiable. It comes up in judgemental senses, as in evaluations of 'our culture' or 'the best culture' when we want to argue something about what we think is right, normal, good, proper, best or highest. It also comes up when we want to refer to the difference of something other. But culture 'itself', if there is such a thing, if there is any kind of physical property, entity, phenomenon, practice or range of phenomena and practices – out there in the world – that could be said to exist as such, 'culture itself' is always elusive: always not quite there and not quite that. There's always more to it than *that* and whichever '*that*' is given as an example of 'culture', it never seems to encapsulate it. 'It' is not 'an it'. Culture is a kind of improper property: you can't quite put your finger on it; it involves an intuition, a sense or an inference.

'Culture' is what the political theorist Ernesto Laclau would call an 'empty signifier': its meaning is up for grabs, and it may well be politically important and consequential who wins the battle over the meaning of the word. Think of a situation in which a political movement defined English culture or British culture or European culture as 'essentially white' or 'essentially Christian'. What does that imply for the status of the others, the non-whites and non-Christians? It consigns them to the status of others, outsiders, welcome or unwelcome guests, intruders or enemies.

As the political philosopher Jacques Rancière might put it, culture is the name of a disagreement. Everyone argues *for culture*, but they mean very different things by 'culture'. Monoculturalists will argue that British culture and society is essentially, naturally or properly white and Christian, so they argue for 'British culture'. Multiculturalists will point out that historically 'British culture' was imposed on all manner of country, colour, creed and context, so these subjects became British during Imperialism and colonialism; or that migration – immigration and emigration – has a long, productive and beneficial history; or that 'they are here' because 'we were there'; or that xenophobic closing of the borders ignores the sociological fact that British culture has long been multicultural – so they argue for 'British culture' too. But both positions mean something entirely different by the word.

Culture is contextual. It is a matter of interpretation. The interpretation is informed by perspective and position, that is by context. But what is 'context'? Jacques Derrida argued that 'context' is something that can never clearly be demarcated. There is always more context to take into account. However, in any case, Raymond Williams points out that 'the history of the idea of culture is a history of our reactions, in thought and feeling, to the changed conditions of our common life' (Williams 1958: 285).[4] For Williams, the key conditions that have influenced the arguments about culture have been industrialisation, democracy and art. The emergence of industrialisation took the form of the industrial revolution's transformation of the social and geographical landscape through the emergence of the city, mass employment in the factory and the foregrounding of class. This had a massive impact. Democracy, as we have already seen, constituted a threat to aristocratic rule and the status quo. It also led to a perceived threat of the danger of individualism and social breakdown, as well as the worrying emergence of an unpredictable mass democracy and mass communications. Finally, transformations and developments in theories and practices of art have informed arguments about culture.

'Art' is traditionally conceived as something to be placed on the side of 'culture' in any kind of 'culture versus *x*' debate – where '*x*' might stand for work, barbarism, capitalism, consumerism, anarchy, the machine or any other supposed opponent to all that is supposed good. But where do we place the media in such a schema? As we have already seen, literature relies on a technological apparatus that is substantially equivalent to the technological apparatus involved in the production and circulation of newspapers, which are traditionally regarded as part of the media. The only difference with literature has been one of *speed*. It has traditionally taken longer to produce a book than a newspaper. But this is a less and less necessary or inevitable difference today. We can see this levelling out of the speed of production and circulation in the case of online publishing, ebooks and ibooks, of course, as well as in some of the publishing industry's range of responses to online publishing, such as the emergence of on-demand physical publishing, in which books are not printed in large batches as they once were, but instead individual machines print, bind and dispense individual copies of books upon demand.

Moreover, certain types of media allow for the dissemination of 'art' (aka 'culture'). And, once again, this inextricability or intertwining of culture and the media or art and the media has long been regarded as a very serious problem by all manner of thinkers of culture and politics It is to the most profound of these that we turn in the next chapter.

2 Media Is (Not) the Culture

Media (and) messages

The media may be many things, but what it is *not* is *clear*. Many possible technologies, processes and institutions could be included in a list of the media. The list is arguably ever-growing. But one thing seems consistent: the media are technologies of *dissemination*. They disseminate signs, sounds, sights, senses and sensibilities. They are widely held to be '*communication* technologies', and they certainly transmit signifiers of various sorts (sounds, words and images).

Nevertheless, I would argue that the word 'dissemination' is preferable to the word 'communication' or the word 'circulation' for describing what the media 'do'. I prefer 'dissemination' even though words like 'circulation' and 'communication' are much more commonly used words in definitions of media processes than 'dissemination'. This is because, as the philosopher Jacques Derrida spent a career trying to point out: no matter what signs or sounds or gestures you or I or a piece of technology emits in an attempt at communication, it is never entirely certain that these things actually 'circulate' intact, unchanged, or that they do actually 'communicate' something successfully. The most that is certain is that they *disseminate* (Derrida 1981).

The fact that Derrida was so widely misunderstood – and indeed, the fact that there is so often dispute and disagreement about the meaning of any text – or at least the fact that Derrida can be so diversely represented, re-represented and misrepresented, perhaps provides the strongest evidence supporting his own argument about the uncertainty of communication. But even though Derrida was definitely difficult to follow in many of his texts (many of which mainly take the form of close readings of already complex philosophers and literary texts – something which obliges us to ask whether *Derrida* is difficult or whether Derrida *reveals the difficulty* of these other texts), it is fair to say that he was clear on the argument of the difficulty and uncertainty of communication.

To try to communicate his argument and its important social and cultural stakes and consequences, Derrida used the example of a postcard (Derrida 1987). We will be able to update Derrida's now quaint-sounding example, and to use a more current example of our own, such as an example like an email, an SMS text message, a blog post, a comment on a website, or some other such type of quick and relatively open form of communication – even though we should understand that any example we use will inevitably come to seem quaint, dated and, ultimately, archaic. Nevertheless, the point is, says Derrida, that a postcard is *legible* to anyone, but it is not necessarily *intelligible* to anyone. You may be on holiday in China, for example, and choose to send a postcard to an old friend in the UK or USA. On the back of the postcard you scribble down a quick message. This perhaps contains witticisms or references to old jokes that you and your friend have shared in times gone by. Then you pay for the postage and post the card. In an ideal world, this postcard will make it to its addressee and your friend will laugh at your humorous message.

But this all relies on several things – things that you cannot necessarily rely on. A message might go astray, argues Derrida: a letter might not reach its intended destination. Derrida means this both literally and figuratively. For, first of all, a letter or postcard sent from China to the UK or USA might go astray. It might never arrive. Hence, communication relies on material technological apparatuses and institutions. To get the message intact and smoothly and reliably from A to B or from A to Z depends upon the stability, reliability and efficiency of all of the apparatuses, machines, institutions, staff, networks and so on that are geographically, physically, legally, nationally, institutionally and perhaps even morally entailed in the delivery. (Everything else might be stable, yet someone might still steal or destroy the letter.)

Alternatively, the letter might not be intelligible. It might be misread. The intended addressee (your old friend) might read what you intended to be received as wit, and take offence, thinking that you are being serious when you intended irony or that you are being grumpy, rude or nasty when you intended to be dry and deadpan. In the way that people sometimes do not 'get' a joke, so sometimes people do not 'get' an intended meaning or effect. And, in the case of the *absence* of the sender, sometimes you can never know *how* something was received or understood. How many times have we sent text messages, emails or instant messages, or commented on other people's posts only to find out later that they or someone else has taken great offence? Of course, we tend to think of all this as a case of 'misreading'. But Derrida's point is that there's no guarantee that anything will be read 'correctly' or as intended. In other words, signs do not necessarily 'circulate' or 'communicate'. They certainly disseminate. They emit. They signify. But there is no guaranteed, ultimate signified or guaranteed meaning.

To make the same point in reverse: if and when a letter or meaning 'reaches' its destination, 'intact', and 'communicates' exactly the signified intended by the sender, then this implies a great deal of stability or predictability: the sender can predict a lot about the receiver. When we come to broaden our interpretation of the postcard example or allegory, when we are no longer talking about one person sending a postcard to another, and when we are instead thinking about *mass media*, this idea – that the sender can predict a lot about the receiver – will come to take on ominous dimensions.

But before we leave the hypothetical postcard example, Derrida adds, the postcard that goes astray, or even the postcard on its way to its destination, may also along the way have been looked at by one or more postal workers. Perhaps the postal worker does not read English at all, so your words will certainly not signify what you intended them to signify. But they will still signify *something*, however 'incorrect', and even if it is little more than 'Ah, this is written in English, I think…Or is that French or Italian?' Moreover, maybe this or that other unintended reader can read English, but does not have any knowledge of you, the sender, the receiver, or your shared points of reference. All the reader has are the marks on the page, and may well be hard put to decide whether the message is serious, light-hearted, aphoristic, code or anything else. Such a reader will be able to *construct* or *invent* an interpretation, or several, but none of them will necessarily be the one you intended – or *think* you intended. For, *even you* may yourself look back later at what you wrote and reflect: 'Did I actually intend that to be a light-hearted joke, or was it actually a snide comment or jibe – before I was even fully aware myself that I was feeling jealous or angry? Was my supposed wit really a sign or symptom of my resentment? Was my wit really innocent, or was I having a dig at the other person?' Sometimes we can look back and realise that, at least at some moments, we have not necessarily been completely aware of our motivations, feelings, resentments, anxieties or worries. In other words, sometimes, at least, perhaps we are not even aware of our own intentions, nor in full control of our own intended meanings.

As well as all of this, there is a more fundamental or material dimension to Derrida's example or allegory: the very existence of the postal network in the first place. It may not *work* properly. It may be faulty, unreliable or corrupt. In other words, its very existence attests to the relative stability of more than one social institution. The very existence of a postal network, a telegraph system, a telephone line or an Internet connection, not to mention the electricity supply that most of these require, indicates the complex interconnectedness of any form of media and a society, within societies and between them. And this interconnectedness has also proven to be something of a worry for theorists and analysts of media and culture.

Interconnectedness, V.1

There are many dystopian views of a present or possible future society. Some of the most enduring hinge on an idea of interconnectedness across all spheres, an interconnection that makes society into either a bureaucratic nightmare (Kafka), a totalitarian surveillance society (Orwell) or an 'engineered' society managed by the 'conditioning' of people from the moment of birth or earlier to be content with their place in life and the sensual and intellectual pleasures appropriate to that place (Huxley). The more or less total interconnection of media, culture, state, social, public and private institutions has been a stock theme of science fiction and conspiracy fiction (and theories) since at least the dawn of the 20th Century, with the proliferation of 'massification' in cities, housing, employment and culture, and the increasingly apparent interconnection of all our lives.

One of the abiding concerns to do with interconnected societies on the part of both fiction writers and philosophers has been related to the apparently increasing power of large forces over our lives, coupled with a diminishing of individuals' or collective groups' *agency*, or power or control. The larger forces have been regarded either as the power of faceless bureaucracy or government or 'the system', or as the power of the enigmatic dictator. In the face of both of these forces, the media are arguably central.

In the wake of the fascism that emerged in the first half of the 20th Century and the Second World War which waged partly as a consequence, many theorists of culture and society noted the instrumental role played by broadcasting technologies, specifically the radio and the cinema, in the emergence and hold of fascism. These media enabled the widespread dissemination of propaganda and also the personality cults around such figures as Stalin, Hitler, Mussolini and, later, Mao – each of whom was constructed as sage and as uncle, as one of the good folk who was yet a superior in wisdom and virtue. Without the radio, the cinema and the press, it has been argued, these figures could not have become such personalities. The cinema, argued Andre Bazin, makes its objects and characters larger than life. So the integration of these three key media – radio, cinema and press – enabled a type of power to emerge that the French theorist Guy Debord called the 'integrated spectacle' (Debord 1990). For, since the emergence of the mass media, argued Debord, societies became 'spectacular' – organised by and around attention to spectacles or media events (Debord 1994). This form of organisation of everyone's attention by the mass media enabled that attention to be directed, and hence directed towards the powerful controlling figures and their messages.

Interconnectedness, V.2

Debord later theorised an even more subtle and sophisticated type of 'spectacular power' (Debord 1990). The society of the spectacle that Debord first theorised, in which people's attention was directed to and by one key force, was not the end of the story. For, later, Debord went on to propose that a 'spectacular logic', or the logic of spectacular domination had transformed and diversified. In his revised account of the society of the spectacle, Debord argues that with the proliferation of media and the saturation of more and more aspects of more and more of our lives by media, the issue is not so much that we are locked into state propaganda as that we are locked into a fascination with image, falsity, insubstantiality, unverifiability, 'noisy insignificance' and consumption. Jean Baudrillard would later pick up this idea and run with it, calling such a media-saturated image society 'hyperreal' (Baudrillard 1994). But for Debord the problem is political: in such a spectacular society, we lose not only 'the real' but also our agency: we become so concerned with 'noisy insignificance' (soaps, game shows, 'reality' TV, celebrity tittle-tattle) and the media merry-go-round turns so fast that we either know nothing of any reality beyond our own TVs and bodies, or what we do hear about serious or significant events vanishes as soon as it falls out of the headlines – which it will do very quickly once it becomes old news and becomes replaced by a newer, fresher, more dramatic scandal.

So, with Debord's influential account, there are two key issues: on the one hand, the media society distracts us from the serious, the real and the important. Behind this, states and powers can operate in secrecy and often with impunity. This much is not new. But also, on the other hand, we are not only distracted by the media; we are ensnared by it; entranced; enthralled; literally, captivated – captured.

Debord himself does not say an awful lot about the daily-life experience of living such a captured life. (And critics have pointed out that, in true Marxist fashion, Debord paints 'us' – or, rather, 'them' – as captured, while he, the critic, somehow escapes capture.) But he builds upon a theme that was perhaps most comprehensively elaborated by the earlier Marxist critics, Theodor Adorno and Max Horkheimer, in 1947. Adorno and Horkheimer's most famous essay of this time is called 'The Culture Industry: Enlightenment as Mass Deception'. It was first a chapter in their 1947 book, *Dialectic of Enlightenment* (Adorno and Horkheimer 1986). In it, Adorno and Horkheimer offer what was then the very new and unusual term, 'the culture industry'. They did this to clarify a distinction between ideas that were currently prevalent about 'mass culture' and their quite new claim about the emergence of what they called a 'culture industry'.

In offering this new oxymoronic term (culture *industry*), they hoped to get rid of the idea that 'mass culture' is something that the masses, the majority of people, here and there, somehow *spontaneously* 'choose'. Rather than this, they argued, 'the culture industry' names a new and complex situation characterised by the *domination* and transformation of everyday culture, everyday life, and hence aspects of our very identities *by a capitalist industry*. In this situation, they suggest, the very ideas of freedom and choice become a mockery – a pale imitation of the real thing.

What is meant by this can be illustrated by looking at a famous early scene of *Fight Club* (1999, Dir David Fincher). In this early scene, we hear a monologue by the protagonist, played by Edward Norton, about the emptiness of his/our everyday life, while we watch him go about his business in his apartment. The camera pans across his living room, as text pops up next to items of furniture, so that it becomes clear that he has bought all of his furniture from a catalogue – from the same catalogue – and that his own 'individual style' and 'taste' has been given to him by one catalogue from one multinational retail chain. This is a pure example of what Adorno and Horkheimer call 'pseudo-individualisation'. We think we are all individuals, but a closer inspection would reveal that we are more or less ensnared by marketing strategies. This means that our individuality is 'pseudo' – not real, not authentic and not arising within us.

Moreover, as we see very clearly in the IKEA scene in *Fight Club*, Norton's character is involved in an empty quest – he pursues it relentlessly, but like a zombie: every time he opens the catalogue he sees that he 'needs' just one more item, just one more set. But of course, this 'need' is neither real, nor satisfiable. Adorno and Horkheimer call it 'a circle of manipulation and retroactive need', and through it, they argue, the hold of 'the iron system' of consumption becomes ever stronger. To use an expression made famous by their colleague, Herbert Marcuse, such people become 'one dimensional': empty, vacuous, aimless herd animals. One of the ironies about Norton's desire in *Fight Club* is that what he is pursuing is not particularly difficult, expensive or unobtainable. It is nothing more than relatively affordable mass-produced commodities for a mass market. Norton's desire is not idiosyncratic, unique, unusual or impossible. It is a desire for the norm, the everyday, the usual. But, as Norton's emptiness and his immanent fascination with violence and destruction reveal, the film suggests that 'the problem' is with this norm itself. It is 'schizophrenic'.

Other films, works of fiction and philosophy have also suggested as much. *Fight Club* is like *American Psycho* (2000, Dir Mary Harron) and other contemporary texts which select a lead character who is the very embodiment of a social 'type' in order to show through their psychic breakdown that the civilisation of which they are a part is itself split or fractured. We will consider this theme further below. But for now let's stick with the important observation that *Fight Club* proposes – in a way that is not too far removed from what Adorno and Horkheimer argued in 1947 – that this *apparently* individual desire and drive is *not* individual or unique. It is a set of aspirations that have been *put* there or engendered. One is not *born* desiring IKEA products.

Norton's character 'ventriloquises' – repeats, reiterates, verbatim – the words of the IKEA catalogue, the words which tell him why he supposedly 'needs' this or that product, and what it will mean, what it will 'say about' him. His character in the film is perhaps an extreme case – an obsessive on the brink of a breakdown – but the question is: are we really that different from him? Are *we* free? Are *we* influenced? If so, by what? Where do *our* desires come from? What do they mean?

The main protagonist in the film *American Psycho* suffers a similar affliction. This film is set in the heyday and highest echelons of 1980s yuppiedom – in the context of conspicuous consumption and the drive for what sociologist Pierre Bourdieu termed 'distinction' – a desire to set oneself *apart* from the crowd, a desire to view oneself as significantly *different* from others. Bourdieu argued that people do not desire to be the *same* as their peers, but rather they desire to establish a *distinction*. This distinction is always established within a delimited context – people rarely desire to be *utterly* different from *everyone* else; rather they will aspire to be different, but within certain limits.

American Psycho dramatises the dynamics of this drive for distinction rather well. It can be seen particularly starkly in a scene featuring a group of corporate vice presidents (every male character in the film appears to be a vice president). These vice presidents are exchanging, comparing and discussing each other's business cards. Barely perceptible differences are regarded as innovations of the utmost magnificence and importance, and the decision about which business card his peers prefer drives the protagonist into a barely controllable rage. In terms of Adorno and Horkheimer's argument about the effects of the culture industry, this scene suggests something about *all* consumption – namely, that it weirdly contorts our values. Irrelevant details and features become important to us – in *American Psycho* they become more important than others' lives.

Elsewhere, Adorno calls this a kind of *fetishism*: capitalist consumption turns us all into fetishists, who 'need' particular details before we can be satisfied. Of course, we can never be satisfied because fetishistic satisfaction is fleeting and not fundamental. Adorno also argues that capitalist consumption – through the things it offers us, the things we get into – causes us to *regress*. We *regress* into fetishism. We become like petulant, spoilt brats, like children attempting to get the biggest or smallest or pinkest or bluest or softest or hardest or whatever-est toy. The detail itself doesn't matter. What matters is that we want what someone else seems to have. The anthropologist René Girard used the psychoanalytic theory of Jacques Lacan and called this the mimetic triangle of desire: we want what we think the other wants/has/is enjoying. But this is what Adorno and Horkheimer propose happens to us in a consumer society: objects become more important than people; a destructive, nihilistic individualism proliferates; and we all become like stupids, horrible spoilt brats – like little fascists.

Both of these films offer strong critiques of consumerism and – by extension – implicit critiques of capitalism. Indeed, both of these films associate consumerism with madness, and specifically, with schizophrenia. The protagonists of both films are profoundly schizophrenic. In this sense, they may be contrasted with – not opposed to: merely contrasted with – films such as *Pretty Woman* (1990, Dir Gary Marshall), for instance, which suggests that whilst capitalism is *ultimately* empty (or, as Jean Baudrillard once put it, that 'the pursuit of objects is without object' – that is, empty, meaningless, vacuous, unsatisfying in and of itself), it is nevertheless a source of immense pleasure, stability and security – just think of the celebrated shopping scene in *Pretty Woman*: haven't we all at one point or another harboured the desire to go out and buy whatever we want, with no limit, with money being no object? *Pretty Woman* plays out this fantasy and tells us that it is indeed great. Consumerism is great.

And, maybe it is. But through this obsession with consumption and distinction, what these scenes also suggest is a relationship between identity and *class*. For, *glamour* is all about *wealth*. The usual representations of glamour always associate 'the most glamorous' (i.e. the 'best') with whatever the richest in society can afford, whatever the richest are buying, wearing and doing. Indeed, even in *The Communist Manifesto*, Marx and Engels noted how 'the ruling ideas of each age have ever been the ideas of its ruling class'. We might say that this is certainly the case here, in the context of ruling ideas of glamour. But *Pretty Woman* adds an extra dimension to this by clearly including gender relationships in the mix: Julia Roberts' prostitute character is trying to be a strong independent woman; Richard Gere's multimillionaire capitalist character is already a strong independent man; but what the film suggests is that neither can be truly happy until they find love. Happy ever after.

Something similar takes place in *Fight Club* too – when Norton's character and Marla walk off together for their happy ever after. In *American Psycho*, on the other hand, Patrick Bateman remains in a miserable state because he cannot escape from his solitary consuming life and find love.

Fight Club begins with the question: 'what does this product say about me?' This draws our attention to advertising's strategies and tactics of infiltrating and organising subjectivity itself. The answer in the film is spoken by Brad Pitt's Tyler Durden character: Tyler says: this and every product – and the act of consumption itself, makes you less of a man. Tyler Durden says 'consumption has feminized masculinity'. In this regard, *Fight Club* dramatises a reactionary rejection of the consumerist and liberal idea of 'the new man', a figure who has been constructed from marketing and media. Consumption, it says, is woman's stuff. Men should fight. *American Psycho*, on the other hand, equates competitive consumption with an all-consuming, envy-fuelled individualism. However, *Pretty Woman* is fairly cut and dried: the upper classes have it good, it says. 'It's all about the money'. These are among the first words you hear in both the film itself and in the trailer for it: 'Welcome to Hollywood' and 'what's your dream?' Upper-class taste is *tasteful* taste. The stuff that rich people like is the best stuff.

This is important, and intimately connected with culture and the media, because what it tells us is that by desiring, say diamonds and pearls and designer labels if and when we can't afford them, what we are doing is identifying with the lifestyle of the upper classes. This is not 'keeping it real'. This is, as you might say, 'living the dream', but not in the sense of making the dream a reality; rather it is so in the sense of dreaming through life. Of course, one of the strongest cultural myths or narratives that organises people's lives takes the form of what most people know as 'the American Dream'. This is the dream of self-creation. There is nothing wrong with it in itself. But the problem comes when this myth becomes translated into a form which means affluence is the ideal. For, in Pierre Bourdieu's terms again, one can only attain distinction if there are others who cannot. Thus, aspiring for the diamond ring or the designer clothes is only going to provide you with your distinction as long as no one else has quite the same thing. But commodities tend not to work like that. Others *will* have them. Aspiring for uniqueness and individuality through commodities is to aspire for what Adorno and Horkheimer again called 'pseudo-individualisation'.

Fight Club proposes the same thing more clearly, if comically: isn't it ridiculous to strive for completion and satisfaction by means of mass commodities, because the set will obviously never be complete? All it can become is obsolete – superseded by a new set, a new range, a new style? Even products that are sold as the 'definitive' version have obsolescence and incompletion built into them.

Interconnectedness, V2.1 (supplement)

A supplementary point related to this matter: a few years ago there was an advert for the definitive and complete *Star Wars* (1977, Dir George Lucas) DVD collection. Obviously, it comprised all of the *Star Wars* films. But, more importantly, the set was said to include a crucial supplement: an extra, definitive *supplementary* DVD with 'extras' on it. This 'extra' supplement is positioned as if it completes the product. But of course, what it actually does is guarantee the *eternal incompletion* of the product. It introduces the need for the collector–consumer to constantly have to update, upgrade, buy, whatever newly definitive 'definitive version' comes on the market next year. *The supplement does not complete. The supplement demonstrates the impossibility of completion.* There can always be another supplement, to update and supplement the old supplement. As Adorno and Horkheimer formulate this, 'The result is the circle of manipulation and retroactive need in which the unity of the system grows ever stronger'. Indeed:

> The culture industry perpetually cheats its consumers of what it perpetually promises. The promissory note which, with its plots and staging, it draws on pleasure is endlessly prolonged; the promise, which is actually all the spectacle consists of, is illusory: all it actually confirms is that the real point will never be reached, that the diner must be satisfied with the menu.
>
> (Adorno and Horkheimer 1986: 139)

Adorno and Horkheimer suggest that many of our supposed 'needs' and certainly our 'wants' do not arise from *nature*, and not even from *culture* (which *could* potentially be a really good thing), but rather from the *culture industry* – which, to them, is a terrible thing. For they contend that the culture industry has some fundamentally worrying effects on us. To see this, we might even consider the example of love. To stay with the films we've been thinking about: all of these Hollywood films either show or strongly suggest that consumerism (and indeed maybe even the entire economic system that drives our world, capitalism) is empty, pointless, destructive and without meaning. Equally, all of them (and very many more films besides) suggest that the true answer to existential questions of identity and desire is to find your happy ever after – a partner. What could be more 'natural'?

But wait. In doing so, are the films therefore suggesting that the world of consumption, commodities and capitalism is 'false', while the 'true', 'natural', 'correct' path to follow is that of the heart? It would seem so. But a first thing to note is that in the *way* they do this, the films are what we might call *patriarchal*, or, more precisely, *heteronormative* – that is, reaffirming the naturalness and rightness of standard norms of heterosexual gender relations. We will say more about gender relations in due course. But at this stage, I want to think about gender relations – and everything else we might meet – in terms of consumption and mediation – the consumption of images in particular.

Adorno and Horkheimer point out, for instance, that the 'love' proffered by the movies is basically commodified in exactly the same way as everything else. This can be formulated as follows in films like *Fight Club* and *Pretty Woman* and many others besides: *if* the system of consumerism, with its insatiable desires and impossible objectives (to get ahead of the game, to get to the right place, and so on) is shown to be the *problem*, then the solution that these films offer is *the finding*

of love – which equals 'the finding of *meaning*'. However, the problem is that the version of such love/meaning/satisfaction/completion
is equally fictional. For a start, even a cursory glance at *Pretty Woman*
suggests that the film 'knows' that it is a fairy tale, and that we the
viewers are being obliged to suspend our disbelief in order to get any
pleasure from it. Therefore, as Adorno and Horkheimer put it, in the
culture industry, 'Love is downgraded to romance'. That is, viewers are
shown and taught about a model of love that is at once formulaic, an
inferior copy of a former reality, and the transformation of a certain
complex passion into a cinematic genre. What is more, the viewer is
actually being denied the true experience of love. As Adorno argues,
the viewer who cries at the love story cries because they have been
allowed to glimpse a life of dramatic and exciting passions, but this
is a life that they themselves are forever denied. Worse, like Pavlov's
famous dogs who salivated whenever they heard a bell ring, because the
dogs had been trained to associate the bell with the imminent arrival of
food, Adorno and Horkheimer propose that in a media-saturated society,
people become trained to react in certain ways when certain formulaic
'buttons' are pushed: to become tense when the music indicates ten-
sion; to overflow with sadness when the music tells us the scene we are
watching is sad; and so on. Adorno calls this the 'masochistic adjustment' of the audience. And what Adorno is ultimately worried about
is that the consumption of mass-media productions softens us up or
primes us to be susceptible to political and ideological manipulation of
all different sorts.

In any case, they contend, the culture industry penetrates deep into
our lives – offering impossible models of how our lives supposedly
should or 'could' be – even though these are childish fairy-tale impos-
sibilities. Indeed, this is maybe one of Adorno and Horkheimer's most
serious accusations about the culture industry – about popular music
and Hollywood film in particular: namely, that it makes us stupid; that
it makes us into drooling, gullible, manipulable cretins, who think and
act like savage little children; or easily swayed proto-fascists.

Shop around

Adorno and Horkheimer have not been the last to connect capitalism
and its consumer culture to fundamental changes in human attitudes and behaviours. For instance, we might merely think about the
expression 'shop around!' It is not uncommon to hear this expression

used in the context of finding a partner. But this formulation may be quite telling, in that it suggests something about the way we have come to think about relationships themselves. For, sometimes, at least, we evidently think of relationships in terms of consumption.

Perhaps we increasingly think of more and more aspects of our lives in terms of consumption. More and more aspects of life are privatised. We are encouraged to 'shop around' in more and more places, realms and registers, across so many different aspects of our lives: for commodities, for places to live, for schools, doctors, utilities, banks, pensions, even lifestyles and belief systems (we are said to 'buy into' particular beliefs); we even now shop around for friends – in what people have called 'the network society'. The term 'network society' is one that used to refer solely to business practices and the world of work. However, increasingly, we now all 'network' (with the word becoming a verb, whereas it was previously exclusively a noun); and increasingly we only want to network with people we think are 'worth it'; people who we think we can 'gain' from; we shop around for 'friends'; for 'communities'; we even shop around for love.

We might think that this is innocent. Haven't we always done this; haven't things always been like this? In one way, maybe yes. But in an other way, perhaps not. As the theorist Jean-François Lyotard once argued, what has increasingly happened since 1945 is that our lives have become increasingly *hegemonised* – dominated and transformed – by the 'penetration of capitalism into language', and by the dissemination of this through increasingly interconnected media. Thus, even if all the old ingredients are all still there, they have been redirected and reorganised in a certain way – like iron filings being redistributed in the presence of a magnetic field. In this transformed context, we increasingly think about life in terms of costs, benefits, investments, profits and losses, and we all want to make a profit – a notion that is extended into more and more areas of life – from commerce, to investments, education, personal relationships, and to ourselves. We invest in ourselves. Thus – at the same time as we approach the world and engage in social relations in terms of consumption (is this, that, he, she or it a good investment for me? Are they worth it? and so on) – many thinkers have pointed out that we have come to *regard ourselves as commodities*. We want to make ourselves the best we can be so others will choose us – will buy us, invest in us and select us.

As well as all the commodities we buy in the hope that they might 'say something about us' – like Edward Norton's character in *Fight Club* – from clothes, music, posters and hairstyles, tocars, houses and furnishings – we choose to go to the right places, do the right things and act in the right way. On the one hand, this is the age-old striving for *distinction* that Pierre Bourdieu first pointed out: our tastes are formed by our contexts, our peer groups, our life-worlds. But on the other hand, it is something quite new when the distinctions we strive for more and more are all taking place in terms of the logic of capitalist exchange – when *what we want to be is a commodity*. For what this suggests is that the penetration of capitalism into more and more aspects of our lives leads us to regard not only everything else and everyone else as 'objects' but also to relate to ourselves as 'objects'.

Thus, the things we desire, the things we want, the things we want to be or be like are never 'subjects' (with a complex subjectivity), but rather 'objects', with certain simple and shared 'objective' features – like a 'design spec'. In other words: *We really do like our coffee like we like our men or women*: pushing the right buttons, conforming to a formula, a template, a type – like a product.

A quick glance at any Lad's Mag or music video will confirm this. A 'content analysis' of the typical features of male or female actors and actresses will demonstrate the increasing hold of not just physical types but also of surgically, cosmetically augmented and altered facial features. In Adorno and Horkheimer's words:

> The culture industry does not sublimate; it represses. By repeatedly exposing the objects of desire, breasts in a clinging sweater or the naked torso of the athletic hero, it only stimulates the unsublimated forepleasure which habitual deprivation has long since reduced to a masochistic semblance. (p. 140)

In other words, for Adorno and Horkheimer, the effects of consuming too many Hollywood films include the following: (1) because there is nothing 'artistic' about them, they make us become like Pavlov's drooling dogs; (2) the culture industry stimulates but represses desire (we have to learn to be satisfied with the menu); thus, ultimately (3) it makes us masochists.

Feminist theorists have long noted the apparent masochism of women. For, what is masochism? In its most simple description, masochism is the taking pleasure from one's own pain. Feminists have characterised femininity as a kind of masochism. For, women take great pains (literally) to look good, right, proper or best. Bodices, basques, lingerie, high heels, make-up, dieting, hair styling, hair dyeing, hair removal – the list goes on and on. Achieving femininity is a lot of work. As Simone de Beauvoir put it, one is not born a woman, one becomes a woman. Femininity is produced. As is masculinity, of course. But if we compare and contrast the two, we can see that historically the production of femininity is a lot more painstaking and a lot more pain. Learning to love high heels, learning to be unable to leave the house or answer the door without a full face of make-up, and many other female obligations, is a lot more painstaking and painful than learning to love beer, swearing, acting tough and playing a bit of sport at the weekend.

Of course, patriarchy has long been operative. Women have long been expected and coerced to become feminine, by internalising the desires and requirements of the patriarchal gaze. – By 'gaze' I mean the implicit point of view that we seem to act in awareness of when we behave in certain ways. Women who enjoy and perform in the most clearly masochistic forms of femininity – the mini-skirt, high heels, impossibly long false nails, are surely good examples here – could be said to be performing for the male gaze. But if Adorno and Horkheimer are to be believed, then it is *both* men and women who are subject to the ravages of the culture industry.

What else do Adorno and Horkheimer suggest those ravages are? First, 'The whole world is made to pass through the filter of the culture industry': it must be *represented*, and that which controls the means of representation is the culture industry. (Real life is becoming indistinguishable from the movies, they say.) Then, the problem of 'pseudo-individualisation'. We all *think* we're individuals, but we're all doing basically the same thing – buying stuff; treating more and more of our relationships as if they were economic relations of production, consumption and exchange; desiring to be commodities ourselves; and objectifying or reifying life into fixed 'types' and 'forms'. Herbert Marcuse (who was Adorno and Horkheimer's colleague) called this the birth of 'one dimensional man'.

Other theorists, including their contemporary Walter Benjamin and our contemporary Slavoj Žižek, have called this a state of 'interpassivity' – namely, the situation in which we all basically 'do stuff' all of the time, but this doing is not really active, it is, rather, basically passive. The argument here is that we are *made passive* by such activities as cinema-going, television-watching and radio-listening. Moreover, these are activities which Adorno and Horkheimer associated with *fascism*, because they are all one-way streets, like the propaganda and control mechanisms of Nazi Germany and Stalinist Russia: these technologies make audiences become used to passively listening to, and accepting messages communicated in a one-way direction, like orders, with little or no reciprocity.

Furthermore, even though the society may be networked and connected, *we* are separated. Our worlds and lives become atomised. We are lone spectators in the crowd of cinemagoers; or we are isolated individuals watching television programmes alone; shopping alone, or driving along in our cars, alone. The later theorist, Guy Debord called this 'separation perfected' – the production of 'lonely crowds' in 'the society of the spectacle'. Debord used the image of mute spectators gazing transfixed at a movie screen as the cover for his infamous book *The Society of the Spectacle* (1967, 1994).

Thus, say Adorno and Horkheimer, in this world dominated by the culture industry, there is no possibility for social or political agency, because we are 'separated' and passive. We have no other 'options' than to pursue our own purposes, individualistically. However, the *way* that the culture industry 'individuates' rather than 'individualises' us makes us all the same, passive, deluded, and unable to think or act properly as individuals or act according to 'culture' or 'politics'. In Adorno and Horkheimer's words: the individual is now 'in social contact with others with whom he has no inward contact'. And: 'the effort to achieve individuation has at last been replaced by the effort to imitate'.

This is not to say that there is no individuality and only a homogeneous mass. Adorno and Horkheimer explicitly disagree with this sort of argument. For them, we really all do think and feel and act like individuals. The problem is that our choices have been mapped out for us in advance. The world of choice is indeed multiple, various and dynamic. But it is, to their mind, a result of 'labelling consumers' in order that, in the system, as they put it: 'Something is provided for all so that none may escape'.

A good example of this can be seen in the film *Minority Report*, in which we see a direct dramatisation of the ways that adverts 'speak' to us, call to us, as if we are individuals, when really we are examples of market-segments. Different sorts of consumers constitute different markets and markets supply different sorts of product for them. In itself, this doesn't sound all that bad. But consider the case of those who want to use cultural or media means and mechanisms to protest or to try to change things.

Media and cultural agency

The cultural theorist Fredric Jameson considered the case of the punk band, *The Clash*. The Clash, like most punk bands, was anarchic, anti-establishment and anti-capitalist. So they wrote protest songs about this. However, what this effort produced was just more commodities: vinyl records, cassette tapes, then, later, CDs and mp3s, along with posters, t-shirts, and all the rest. What or where is the anti-capitalism in this? What is anti-systemic? There is nothing *necessarily* anti-establishment about spiky hair, peroxide, henna, safety-pins, tattoos, anarchy symbols or swastikas, combat pants, big boots and the rest of punk paraphernalia – especially not when all of this is available as part of a culture industry. The comedian Bill Hicks satirised this very nicely with his lambasting of marketing and advertising, and specifically of marketers who see marketing opportunities even in anti-marketing positions. Through his comedy sketch, Bill Hicks very concisely conjures up the problems of 'rejecting' or 'protesting' 'the system': it may well be all encompassing.

This is an ethos that is shared by many. The very name of the band *Rage Against The Machine* suggests that there is a 'system' – a 'machine' – which ought to be raged against. *Rage against The Machine* had quite a hit with the song 'Bullet in the Head' (1992) – a song which associates watching TV with making us stupid: they speak of the 'in house drive by' – as if the TV is like a gang member shooting us – putting a 'bullet in your head' – that is, making you stupid, passive, inert, docile, subdued and 'comatose'. Bill Hicks expresses the same sentiment in his take on the effect of *American Gladiators* (1989–97). Even Adorno once wrote 'every visit to the cinema leaves me – despite all my vigilance – stupider and worse'.

Nevertheless, for people who so hated the Hollywood film industry and the American popular music industry, Adorno and Horkheimer certainly spent an awful lot of time and energy viewing and listening. So much so that they have come to remind me very much of Waldorf and Statler from *The Muppet Show* (1976–81, Jim Henson) – the two grumpy old men in the box who always claimed to hate the show and who yet nevertheless return every week, religiously. What Adorno and Horkheimer were worried about, though, was this. They were writing in the immediate aftermath of the Second World War. They had fled the Nazis in Germany, and ended up in the USA. They were Marxist intellectuals, Members of 'Frankfurt School' (along with other famous including Walter Benjamin and Herbert Marcuse). They were writing in full awareness of the Holocaust. Fascism was a very real part of their lives. And, sitting in America, watching American culture develop, they were deeply concerned that America – which might be thought to be utterly different from fascism and totalitarianism – might be developing into a different but related sort of monstrous power.

The nature of this power was one in which 'culture' was being stolen and perverted by 'industry'. The 'culture industry' was becoming 'a system which is uniform as a whole and in every part', and in which everything, 'Even the aesthetic activities of political opposites are one in their enthusiastic obedience to the rhythm of the iron system' – And even 'city housing projects designed to perpetuate the individual as a supposedly independent unit' – all of these realms were being increasingly dominated by a capitalist logic.

However, while there is of course an industrial dimension to culture – and while the term 'culture industry' and 'cultural industries' are now often used not in pejorative and outraged terms (to Adorno and Horkheimer, the very combination of the two words 'culture' and 'industry' was an offensive oxymoron) – there is more to our lives and to our cultures than industry. We can see this, for example, in the film *High Fidelity* (2000, Dir Stephen Frears), a film set in the context of the life of a record shop owner and his colleagues who are obsessed with records and music. Their lives are variously and dynamically organised by music – specifically, vinyl records. But, importantly, they each organise their lives and their records differently. The key point to be garnered here relates to the ways that commodities can be variously and dynamically *used*. People relate to commodities differently and do different things with them. Commodities are bound up in identity. Lives can be structured through them. On the one hand we might be 'victims' of them, but on the other hand, we use them, incorporate them into our lives; live our lives through them in any number of different ways. We might consider the scene in which John Cusack's character reorders his records – in terms of the events of his life. As Stuart Hall put it in his famous essay 'Notes on deconstructing "the popular" ':

The meaning of a cultural form and its place or position in the cultural field is *not* inscribed inside its form. Nor is its position fixed once and forever. This year's radical symbol or slogan will be neutralised into next year's fashion; the year after, it will be the object of a profound cultural nostalgia. Today's rebel folksinger ends up, tomorrow, on the cover of *The Observer* colour magazine. The meaning of a cultural symbol is given in part by the social field into which it is incorporated, the practices with which it articulates and is made to resonate. What matters is *not* the intrinsic or historically fixed objects of culture, but the state of play in cultural relations: to put it bluntly and in an over-simplified form – what counts is the class struggle in and over culture.

(Hall 1994: 484)

With this argument, Hall introduces a line of thinking that came to characterise cultural studies – one which acknowledges the forces and power of all manner of different entities and agencies but which does not regard any one as *necessarily* determinant in the last instance. Things are much more complex, processual, and indeed, no matter how interconnected – in fact, precisely because of the degree of the interconnectedness of things – fragmented.

Interconnectedness V3: Disconnectedness

The paradoxical idea that culture becomes more fragmented the more it becomes interconnected by media and other technologies arrives in the historical period known as modernity. It is certainly explored through the modernist art of this period. This is because, what was looming large and ominously over this period is the new and complex phenomenon of the urban landscape – the modern city. The modern city is internally interconnected with roads, walkways, arcades, elevators, escalators, telephone wires, postal networks, tram, train and bus routes and broadcast signals and channels of many orders. Moreover, it is externally interconnected to the rest of the world. And what arises in this densely interconnected environment is not intimacy but rather alienation and even loneliness. In the teeming metropolises of modernity, we have often alienated 'lonely crowds' of isolated individuals.

Modernity came to be associated with the first half of the 20th Century. After the Second World War, and especially after the 1950s, many historians and cultural theorists proposed that Western cities and cultures in particular moved into the era of postmodernity. Postmodernity the historical period is to be distinguished from postmodernism. Postmodernism is or was first and foremost an intellectual and artistic movement, which arose in response to modernism. However, thinkers like Fredric Jameson propose that postmodernism is also an appropriate name for the cultural style of life in postmodernity.

Therefore, postmoder*nity* is a historical period. Postmodernity the historical period is generally identified as starting after the Second World War; generally deemed to be specific to the West, or rather, to urbanised and consumerist societies (which, historically, were classified as 'West', even when they are hardly simply West, like Hong Kong, Tokyo or Sydney); and characterised by a hell of a lot of *choice*. The proliferation of primarily consumption-based choice is deemed to have profound effects on individuals, on cultures and on societies. For, with the proliferation of 'life-style' choices in postmodernity, one can 'buy into' and/or 'perform' any of many religions (Christianity, Islam, Judaism, Buddhism, Hinduism, Sikhism, Taoism, Shinto and so on); identities are said to become fluid or hybrid; travel, migration, cosmopolitanism and travel proliferate; and a diversity of lifestyles and values emerge.

Because of the inescapability and proliferation of 'choice', postmodernism and postmodernity are said to have certain characteristic features. Fredric Jameson writes about what he calls 'The Cultural Logic of Late Capitalism'. Postmodernity, the historical period, he proposes, is defined by consumption in a post-industrial context. Postmodernism, the cultural style of postmodernity, is characterised by inter-textuality (or the inevitable quoting from and alluding to other texts in any 'new' cultural production), irony, pastiche, genre blurring, bricolage, iconoclasm, plurality and the 'rejection of grand narratives.

The rejection of – or incredulity towards – 'grand narratives' is born from the fact that more and more people in a media-saturated culture are aware of the existence of different 'grand narratives' – religious, ideological and so on. And this awareness that traditions are really rather local and parochial leads to a waning of belief in them. People, therefore, treat traditional material ironically – for example, quoting religious or scientific ideas but in such a way that our incredulity before them is obvious ('fundamentalist Christians are surely the most forgiving' or 'science can solve all of our problems').

However, many scholars have pointed out that although our media-saturated 'democratic' societies are indeed filled with choice and competing stories and narratives about truth and value, this does not necessarily mean that grand narratives (or meta-narratives) as such are on the decline. Michael A. Peters, for instance, follows the French philosopher Gilles Deleuze to dispute the postmodernist claim that master-, grand- or meta-narratives are on the wane. Rather, he suggests, 'in the Western world we have witnessed the revival and revitalisation of the master narrative of classical economic liberalism in the guise of neoliberalism' (MP, 115). He continues: 'In a very real sense...neoliberalism represents a heightening and renewal of modernity's dominant metanarrative' (Peters 2001: 119). It is the ideology of 'individualism' (121–134) that bolsters neoliberal capitalism.

Slavoj Žižek too comments on the ideology of 'freedom' and 'liberalism' – in other words, the dominant mantra that we are all ultimately free. Žižek does not accept this as a simply self-evidently true idea. Indeed, with this idea (that we are 'free', that we have 'choice'), Žižek contends:

> Here we are at the very nerve center of the liberal ideology: freedom of choice, grounded in the notion of the 'psychological' subject endowed with propensities he or she strives to realize. This especially holds today, in the era of what sociologists like Ulrich Beck call 'risk society', when the ruling ideology endeavors to sell us the insecurity caused by the dismantling of the Welfare State as the opportunity for new freedoms: you have to change jobs every year, relying on short-term contracts instead of long-term stable appointment. Why not see it as the liberation from the constraints of a fixed job, as the chance to reinvent yourself again and again, to become aware of and realize hidden potentials of your personality? You can no longer rely on the standard health insurance and retirement plan, so that you have to opt for additional coverage for which you have to pay. Why not perceive it as an additional opportunity to choose: either better life now or long-term security? And if this predicament causes you anxiety, the postmodern or 'second modernity' ideologist will immediately accuse you of being unable to assume full freedom, of the 'escape from freedom', of the immature sticking to old stable forms ... Even better, when this is inscribed into the ideology of the subject as the psychological individual pregnant with natural abilities and tendencies, then I as it were automatically interpret all these changes as the result of my personality, not as the result of me being thrown around by market forces.
>
> (Žižek 2001: 116)

In other words, while we may *think* that we are free, while we may feel disconnected, we are all actually connected insofar as we are subject to larger socio-economic processes. But arguably, the issue runs deeper than even Žižek shows it to be here. For what Žižek draws our attention to is the way that ideological messages can be shown to be unreliable – in fact, often opposite to the reality of the situation. And Žižek focuses on the way ideology serves as a kind of 'coping mechanism' for people who have to tell themselves that they are in control when in fact they are being tossed about by the forces of deregulated capitalism.

But other thinkers have drawn attention to the way that, even if the large-scale processes of the global and national economies can be experienced as very chaotic processes, there are nevertheless other means by which we are complexly interlinked and interconnected in media-saturated cultures. Michael A. Peters uses the influential work of the seminal thinkers Michel Foucault and Gilles Deleuze to argue that today's culture is dominated by 'perpetual training' (Peters 2001: 98), everything is turned into a business (105), and, to quote Deleuze (and to echo the Frankfurt School), 'the only people left are administrators' (106). In this perspective, today there is 'no practice of domination other than that of a purely immanent social control by universal marketing in continuous variation and modulation (with the 3 M's ruling the New International Order: Money, Media and Military)' (107).

Gilles Deleuze's argument is a philosophical one, built on the historical and theoretical work of Michel Foucault. Foucault (1926 84) was a historian who developed new insights into the way power works, at every level of culture and society. As Foucault famously argued:

Power...is never localized here or there, never in anybody's hands, never appropriated as a commodity or place of wealth. Power is employed and exercised through a net-like organization...In fact, it is already one of the prime effects of power that certain bodies, certain gestures, certain discourses, certain desires come to be identified and constituted as individuals....The individual is an effect of power, and at the same time, or precisely to the extent to which it is that effect, it is the element of its articulation.

(Foucault 1980: 98)

This is a complex argument, but basically Foucault studied many of the ways by which we are 'made' as useful and productive and predictable members of a society. These include disciplinary mechanisms, like school, education, and examination; physical training of all sorts; and – ultimately – being subject to different sorts of *gaze*.

The gaze in Foucault is connected closely to media. But first it is a matter of surveillance: the parent, teacher, supervisor or warder watches, supervises and examines, and this process of supervising produces effects. Children behave under the teacher's gaze; prisoners behave when they know they are being looked at. Students behave when they know that they are being examined. They pay attention when lecturers talk about assessment. They knuckle down and follow the commands when they hear how to pass exams. So, in this sense, the gaze produces behaviour.

It also produces 'subjects'. The student who wants to pass an exam wants to pass it to get a qualification which can be looked at and understood as a qualification to do or to be something or someone. The student may want a degree because having it is a precondition to entrance into a profession, for example. This means that the gazers at the school are also the servicers of the examination institution, and the examination result provides a certificate which is looked at by the gate-keepers of the profession to decide whether to allow access. So social certification is related to position. And it is all organised by different forms of 'gaze'. The person certificated with a PhD or professorship or mastership of some profession is then an 'effect of power', to use Foucault's words.

Disciplinary gazes are used to discipline us. Policing or securitising gazes are used to police us. There are different sorts of gaze. None can ultimately be divorced from power. The gaze of the teacher or even parent is certainly more complex than the inhuman 'gaze' of a police surveillance camera. But nevertheless, there is at least one sense in which the intended effects of both forms of gaze are not unrelated. They are certainly all interconnected with the question of power.

Surveillance is not the end of the story of the gaze. But it is certainly a large part of the uses of new media technologies today. For instance, London is reportedly the most CCTV-saturated city in the world. Intense and extensive use of surveillance is largely accepted in the UK. But more than this, ID cards, social security numbers, DNA databases and so on, all record our 'identities'. Supermarket Loyalty Cards 'watch' us and record our activities, in order to provide information to marketers about our tastes. Swipe cards, public transport credit cards, financial debit and credit card transactions, among many other things all also account for our activities and movements. Mobile phones and GPS navigation systems transmit our whereabouts. Email systems often automatically 'read' your emails, and use that reading to select 'relevant' 'targeted' adverts to appear on the page next to your conversations.

In these senses, privacy itself is compromised at the same time as we 'naturalise' – internalise, normalise, accept and even justify these intrusions. Of course, this kind of power always has two 'reasonable' alibis/justifications: first, there are always 'good reasons' for surveillance; second, there are always 'bad people' to catch. Such justifications as these for the intrusion of media surveillance mechanisms and networks into the most intimate areas of our daily lives abound. In Chapter 3, we will look at some problematic aspects of the interconnections of media and culture related to this.

3 Media Representation and Its Cultural Consequences

Editing culture: From trivia to tradition

I have long been a student of martial arts. My interest in martial arts was entirely inspired by the films I viewed as a child. This itself is a clear case of the influence of media on culture. But it is not the first thing I want to focus on here. I have done so at length elsewhere (Bowman 2010). Rather than dealing with the connections between film-viewing and personal identity, just yet, I want to tell a story about a recent event, one that relates only incidentally to martial arts but primarily to some important aspects of culture and the media related to filming, editing, selecting and organising media materials into texts. It is this.

One evening, while training, my instructor told me to put on the gloves and throw a few gentle jabs at him. He passed his iPhone to a fellow student and instructed him to film the proceedings. I threw a jab and he immediately intercepted it, simultaneously stepping in close to me and throwing me, in one deft movement. He asked me to repeat the process. I did so several times. On each jab, he would intercept, deflect or parry while stepping inside and going in for a throw, a lock or a choke. This was a very interesting process, and at the time it was clearly a demonstration of variations of a technique unique to a Chinese martial art called *Xing-I*. I was happy to have been filmed, even if I always ended up on the ground, because I anticipated that the end result would be a helpful instructional video, uploaded to YouTube or shared with a group of interested martial artists.

However, the next day, what appeared online for all the world to see was not a clearly labelled training film, but rather a film called 'light sparring'. What was now a neatly edited film was made up from a montage of clips in which I could be seen throwing jabs and then being immediately and dramatically countered in various decisive ways. Even then, I thought little of it. This changed when people started commenting on the 'light sparring' video. 'Bad footwork', they said, about me; 'weak techniques'. 'The puncher is weak'; 'the other guy is really good', they continued. I remonstrated that this was not actually a video of 'light sparring' at all, and therefore my footwork and my technique were entirely irrelevant. I wasn't really trying to fight. I wasn't really trying to punch. But it didn't make any difference. 'What you need to do is . . .'; 'you should have . . .'; 'you need to . . .' – the comments continued. No one heard, noticed, acknowledged or took seriously my point that the video was not what it seemed, not what it purported to be, not in fact a video of 'light sparring' at all. It *seemed* to be a collection of moments from a bout of light sparring. This is in fact what it had been made to seem to be, thanks to the title 'light sparring'. But it was not and had never been a film of 'sparring'.

Needless to say, I soon came to feel quite aggrieved. The fact that my instructor *could* have beaten me just as comprehensively, dramatically and decisively if we had *really* been sparring was not my point. My point was that the episode was – and *I* was – entirely misrepresented. What people *thought* they were seeing was not what they were watching. *The representation itself was a representation of something that had never happened.* There had been no sparring, light or otherwise. And yet there seemed to have been.

Such is the power of representation. And such is its unreliability. Representations claim to be *re*-presentations – the making present *again* of something that *was* present but is no longer present. Yet, as my anecdote hopefully illustrates, representations can also quite easily seem to make something present even if it was *never* there. This troubling potential in the structure of representation itself obviously has potentially significant implications. History is littered with shameful misrepresentations of whole groups, cultures, peoples: the Nazi propaganda representation of Jews as demonic monsters, or of Jazz music as the music of black monkey-like Jewish monsters, for instance, is but one set of stark examples.

Other famous cases include European and Euro-American representations of Africa and Africans, Native Americans, Asians and others, as essentially different and inferior to white Europeans. Like stereotypes, all kinds of misrepresentations, such as what Rey Chow calls the 'fantastic figures of the Jew, the Jap, and the wetback have all produced substantive political consequences, from deportation to incarceration to genocide or ethnic cleansing' (Chow 1995: 59).

Of course, not all representations – not even stereotypes – are straightforwardly negative. Take my own interest in 'Eastern' martial arts, for example: yes, it was born because of, and has always been directly or indirectly routed through nothing other than the often simplistic representations, narratives, fantasies, discourses, constructions and ideologies found in films. But still, my interests in Oriental martial arts and Oriental philosophy remains genuine, no matter how dubious the representations of the things that hooked my interest in the first place may be.

Mediatised ideas, mediatised bodies

This also suggests that even physical practices, such as martial arts training, are inextricably entangled with issues related to media and culture. Indeed, perhaps it is not possible deal 'directly' with martial arts or Oriental philosophy in the contemporary world without dealing with aspects of film, fantasy, Western discourse and ideology. This is because our access to, understanding of, and involvement with either of these two things – martial arts and Oriental philosophy – and *especially* in their conjunction – is always and already informed and organised by *media representations, historical discourses* and *filmic fantasies*. In my case, it was filmic fantasies and their myths and legends about 'what martial artists could do' that first seized hold of my primary-school-aged soul in the 1970s, in the immediate context of what cultural historians call 'the kung fu craze', which peaked (or exploded) with the films of Bruce Lee in 1973. As such, the filmic fantasy that seized my soul was, of course, deeply *Orientalist*, through and through. As the caricatural Chinese Shaolin kung fu martial arts master said to the ridiculously Orientalised David Carradine in the TV series *Kung Fu* (1972–75, Dir Ed Spielman, Jerry Thorpe, Herman Miller), 'Ah, grasshopper!' – and this, as many commentators have pointed out, is itself a kind of representational violence: a simplifying reduction of the other culture to something caricatural, quaint, novel or bizarre, by way of simplistic stereotypes.

'Orientalism' is a term coined by Edward Said to describe the overwhelming tendency of European and American to representation the people and places of the East according to stock stereotypes. 'Orientalism' is not simple racism: it need not be hostile. Images that represent the Orient as mystical or desirable can also be Orientalist, to the extent that they use stereotypical imagery. (Said 1995)

So, my situation is like this: like many others, my interest and involvement in something *bodily* came directly through *filmic* mediation or simulation, and my interest in Oriental philosophy started absolutely from Orientalist fantasy, stereotype and reductive representations of a certain type of alterity. By 'Orientalism' I am using Edward Said's term for the complex of ways in which Europe and its various discourses have 'othered' this or that other country, culture or people; the ways in which Europeans have constructed *an*-other as 'other', and sometimes *the*-other.

Said tells us that his own starting point was his perception of a disjunction: the representations of the Middle East that he saw in the West did not square with his knowledge and experience of the Middle East. Ultimately, he came to argue, it is eminently possible to see that Western discourses have overwhelmingly tended to *project* a lot onto the other culture, to reductively misrepresent it, and to make it seem to conform to prejudicial stereotypes. Not all of these stereotypes are simply negative. Orientalism is not simple racism. For there can be the good 'other' and the bad 'other', the desirable 'other' and the terrifying 'other', the intriguing 'other' and the repellent 'other' and so on. Said refers to this as splitting and doubling: there is the superlatively good other and the superlatively bad other. But both forms amount to the same thing: the invention of an alterity, through the production of a differential, a division between them and us, and the constructing of 'them' as an-other through a reductive simplification.

Said finds a remarkable consistency in the types of things that have been projected onto the Eastern Other by European discourses, throughout history. The other culture becomes represented as everything that the familiar culture is not: so, representations of the outside of Europe construct that other place and its other people as fascinating/terrifying, spiritual/animalistic, sensual/violent, mysterious/childlike, wise/naïve, ancient/spontaneous, traditional/free, state-of-nature/state-of-decadence or whatever.

Western popular cultural handlings of Oriental martial arts have from the outset been Orientalist in this regard. The Asian martial artist is one or another stock figure who is held to be able to perform the most remarkable of physical feats, and to be able to do this with an amazing calmness and almost tranquil equanimity, and to have been able to achieve this state and execute these feats because of his or her dedication to a philosophy that demands exquisite physical discipline, or a physical discipline informed by a philosophy. This Oriental martial-arts philosophy is identified with either/or/both Taoism and/or Chan or Zen Buddhism.

Popular mythology has it that Chinese martial arts arose as such in the Shaolin Temple as a result of the physical training required to master Zen meditation. The legend goes that a monk called Daruma or Bodhidharma came to China from India and devised a series of exercises to strengthen the bodies and minds of the Buddhist monks so that they could endure the harrowing new discipline of Zen meditation. From this conjunction of disciplines, the monks became physically formidable. And so on.

But these are myths and legends. As such, they are of dubious status. Nevertheless, thanks to their mediation, they inform people's beliefs and attitudes. They provide a *fantasy*. Fantasy is a psychoanalytical term that I have a lot of time for. It is not unrelated to the idea of 'belief'. But what is specifically meant by fantasy here comes from Lacan via 1980s cultural theory (from Kaja Silverman at the start to Slavoj Žižek at the end), and it refers to a kind of basic or fundamental scenario that becomes the matrix or paradigm within which the world and ourselves make sense and function, in our own heads. So this is kind of a belief system, but it is one that we aren't necessarily aware of, and it governs the structure of our orientations, interpretations and perspectives. So, our fantasies, through which we imagine how the world works or how we work, can be regarded as fundamental beliefs; beliefs that are so intimate to us that we may not even be aware of them. They are like little algorithms, and they are often very simple, very childish. According to psychoanalysis, this is because we formulated them when we were children.

(Sometimes it is possible to look at people and deduce from their consistencies what their fantasy structure seems to be. I am fairly certain, for instance, that one of my male relatives' fantasy structure is most like the symbolic structure of the 1980s Sylvester Stallone film *Rambo* (1985, Dir George P. Cosmatos), namely, patriarchal, militaristic, individualist and survivalist. He sees himself as a kind of Rambo, and the world or symbolic universe he inhabits is that of this kind of action film, waiting to happen. I sometimes think that my own fantasy structure has the contours of Bruce Lee's put-upon and ultimately doomed quest for justice in *Fist of Fury* (*Jing Wu Men*) (1972, Dir Lo Wei), or indeed Sonny Chiba's embittered Oedipally entangled character in his 1970s *Street Fighter* (1974, Dir Shigehiro Ozawa) films. But mostly I have come to think that my own is closer to the first *Karate Kid* (1984, Dir John G. Avildsen) film, in which the bullied Danny Laruso is rescued, protected and trained by the authentic native informant expert, Mr Miyagi. In short, my fantasy makes my life more like a training film. Faced with the threat of physical violence, I go off and train. And, when pounding the punchbag, many times I have found myself wondering who it was that I should just have hit in the first place so that I didn't have to keep hitting the punchbag; who I should just have fought so that I didn't need to keep training for a fight. In the film *Fight Club*, Brad Pitt's character (who is the schizophrenic fantasy projection of the lead character, played by Edward Norton – the fantasy projection of the ideal man, the man that Norton most fundamentally desires to be – and who, significantly models his fighting style on Bruce Lee's famous moves), Tyler Durden, proposes that the person he'd most like to fight would have to be his own father.)

The point is that the 'intrusion' of media and cultural influences into our minds and bodies through their organisation of our beliefs and fantasies demonstrates one way in which one cannot dissociate media and culture – or, more specifically, *representation as such* – from even the most intimate aspects of our lives and likes, loves and hates. But, of course, the power of representation should not be regarded either as a purely personal matter or as something consigned to 'harmless' matters of cultural taste. Examples of the power of partial, biased or tendentious (mis)representations abound, and on an ongoing and even daily basis, in all manner of contexts and scenes. This is perhaps never more apparent than in and around political issues, debates, protests and events, which, more and more, are 'mediatised'. Consider the following example, which focuses less on the relationship between media and personal predilections and more on the relationship between media processes (selection, bias, editing and hierarchising) and political processes.

Mediatised politics

In November 2010, the UK saw a number of protests in response to the government announcement of spending cuts. According to the TV news, violence apparently occurred during many of these protests. However, there was a competition between at least two opposing ways of representing or interpreting this violence. The dominant approach took the form of claiming that the protestors themselves were violent. The opposite approach took the form of claiming that the police had at least courted or perhaps provoked, forced, conducted or even orchestrated the violence. These latter claims focused on the newly named police tactic of 'kettling' protestors – that is, containing them within confined spaces, for any length of time and for any number of purported reasons.

If media representation is as unreliable as I began this chapter by suggesting, let me therefore propose at the outset that – like many things in a mediated world, a world reliant upon representation – we cannot simply know for sure what happened everywhere in and around the protests. So rather than focusing on trying to 'objectively' establish this, let us instead start from a different angle, in order to explore the significance of a mediatised society for culture and politics. In fact, it will be my contention here that remembering the central place and problems of media representation will help us a great deal in understanding contemporary *society* and *cultural/political processes* – and not just in understanding contemporary *media*.

Violent demonstration: A mediatised logic

Despite being couched by much media, political and especially official government rhetoric as being entirely inexplicable, it was perhaps eminently possible to understand the 'violence' that took place during the so-called student demonstrations in London during the winter of 2010–11. This violence was initially reported as being the violence of the protestors. However, thanks to the recording and dissemination technologies of mobile phones, smart phones and platforms such as YouTube, FlickR and Twitter, many videos quickly came to light which suggested in various ways that much if not all of the violence and disturbance was quite possibly provoked by the tactics of the police themselves (see BBC 2010; Guardian 2010).

Of course, in a sense, it may be relatively easy to understand any government's desire to recast any *police* violence as the *violence of the protestors* (Lenin 2010). But what was slightly more perplexing in the case of 2010 was the kind of sustained media representational 'violence' in this discourse. This 'violence' was of a different order to that of the hands-on 'policing' of the police themselves and that of the 'political policing' of the discourse about the protests (i.e. the striving of politicians to represent the events in certain tendentious ways). We will return to questions of such 'media' – or representational – 'violence' (bias, selectivity, exclusion and so on) in due course. But first, it seems worthy of note that the police violence itself could actually be said to operate according to a media (or mediatised) logic.

This can be seen in the realisation that there was an obvious police strategy which hinged on the decisions about *where* to 'kettle' (contain) people (McQuillan 2010a). It became clear quite early on that the kettles (zones of containment) were often set for the most dramatic media effect. The logic seemed to be as follows: 'Kettle protesters there, so that when they start to boil, they will daub graffiti on *this* monument, light fires with *this* treasured material and smash *these* particular windows'. This becomes a perfect process for demonising the freezing, frustrated, angry protestors, 'showing' them to be violent vandals. This is similar to the much publicised event of the police abandoning a police vehicle right in the middle of one demonstration. The idea in that case now seems obvious: let the demonstrators smash it up, so that plenty of footage of the protestors attacking the police and vandalising the police van could be produced. Thankfully, a group of 16-year-old schoolchildren saw through this tactic and actually started protecting the police van from vandalism (YouTube 2010).

Given the proliferation of these sorts of events, it seems likely that the strategists behind such 'mediatised policing' were evidently quite clear about what they intended to do. The aim of all policing – it almost goes without saying – is to maintain the status quo; and from such a perspective, the ends might often easily seem to justify the means. So, from such a perspective, it can easily 'make sense' both to demonise and to try to deter protests and protestors. Media images are crucial here. These help to make sure that protests are regarded (because represented) as scary, violent affairs, associated with criminality, irrationality and danger. Such a representation is likely to help to deter potential challenges in future and also to pre-empt and undermine future protests (by strengthening the hold of a 'pre-digested' interpretation of protests as bad, criminal and/or futile).

Moreover, from a policing point of view, there is never enough policing anyway, and there can never be enough. There are always 'threats'. So it makes sense – even at the risk of attracting some bad press – to test the boundaries of what passes as acceptable policing practice. Push the envelope; kettle, charge and punch the protestors (Blip.TV 2010). That is to say: *each demonstration is equally (or reciprocally) at the same time a demonstration of police power, and therefore also an experiment in what can be practiced and normalised.* For strategists in charge of policing, there is a logic: there can never be enough security. Therefore, for them demonstrations mean exceptionalism – a claim of exceptional circumstances demanding exceptional practices. Anything constructed as a 'state of exception' can be used to try to justify any exceptional violence – especially in the context of spectacular media images of protests as anti-police, anti-status quo and violent or criminal.

Moreover, we should also note: the police force itself was also facing budget cuts. So anything that the police could do to demonstrate their own necessity and to 'show' the need to expand investment in the police force rather than cut it back is surely understandable. The police force always needs criminals, and plenty of them – good, dramatic, visible ones too; ones that need lots of police to police them. This police logic quickly started working: soon after the 'student protests', the Home Secretary gave explicit approval for the use of water canon on future protests.

And finally, as a footnote to the logic of the media spectacle in play here, it also needs to be clear that the intensive physical policing seen during the political protests of the winter of 2010–11 always also operated as a means to enable an enormous amount of data-gathering, information gathering, surveillance and scrutiny. Everyone who wanted to leave a kettle (i.e. everyone) was only allowed to leave after being photographed, fingerprinted and comprehensively ID-ed.

As mentioned earlier, though, what remained much less explicable throughout the protest period was a kind of sustained 'media violence' in the form of the persistence of representing the protests as 'riots', riots that were simply spontaneously 'caused' by the violent intentions of the protestors; the persistence of framing the protests as inherently violent; of focusing on minor acts of vandalism rather than the simple reasons for the protestors being stuck there in the first place; the violence of representing the protests as purely student-interest, as selfish, as merely a matter of self and selfishness; and the complete ignoring of the political logic of the shocking responses, on the streets, in Parliament and, worse, in the media itself.

Demonstrations of violence

The philosopher Jacques Rancière argues that politics is essentially quite rare. This is because, according to Rancière, politics only happens when there is a social convulsion – a kind of performative debate about the *status* of some-one or some-group or some-thing within the community. Thus, vis-à-vis feminism, for example, the domestic kitchen became political not simply because there are power relations there. There are power relations everywhere. Rather, at a certain point in time, the domestic kitchen became political because there was a wider social debate about the status of women in the community (Rancière 1999).

There was a sense at the time that the student protests about the cuts to education proposed by the Conservative-Democratic (or Con-Dem) Coalition were spearheading a wider political convulsion in the UK in Rancière's sense. Moreover, after the UK's Winter of Discontent, and after the Arab Spring of 2011, in the summer heat of August 2011, London and other major cities in the UK became consumed by large-scale rioting for several consecutive days and nights. Commentators from the status quo dismissed them as 'pure criminality'. UK Home Secretary Theresa May used this expression repeatedly in her initial reactions. Prime Minister David Cameron described the riots as 'utterly unacceptable'. Others, however – including rioters who were interviewed by various journalists – instead connected this upsurge and outpouring of anger and destruction to the effects of economic recession and the cuts implemented with such ruthlessness and alacrity by the Conservative-Democratic Coalition (Con-Dem) Government (Red 2011).

If media images of looting worked to support the perspective of the Con-Dem Government (insofar as stealing trainers and computers from shops hardly seems to be a properly political gesture), the spontaneity and widespread character of the riots would tend to complicate interpretations. After all, unless all teenagers are all latent criminals who would spontaneously do *anything* if they thought they would get away with it (as, in fact, the dominant economico-psychologistic theory preferred by neoliberal thinkers, academics and ideologues – 'rational choice theory' – would actually tend to suggest), it is not clear how easy it would be actually to start a riot in a period or area of calm or prosperity or harmony, or to have a riot that would provoke unconnected regions and areas to join in with 'copycat' self-destruction.

So there are questions about what all or any of this teaches, or what there is to be learned. What can be learned from mediatised popular culture? An older set of paradigms, infused with Marxism, have focused on conjunctural analyses which explain behaviours and issues in terms of conjunctures: political and economic forces precipitating in events. According to this approach, government cuts in a time of recession will amplify inequality, alienation, disenfranchisement, resentment and frustration. Society is always latently and often becomes explicitly racialised. The forms and contours of racialisation can be mapped onto lines of class antagonism. Unemployed youth are all too easily criminalised. Criminality is all too easily racialised. Police logic remains obdurately 'institutionally racist'. Media discourses feed on spectacles and bespeak hegemonic values. So, social and cultural convulsions are represented as inexplicable spectacles perpetrated by the scary irrational criminal underclass and so on. This much we 'know'.

However, is this really a 'knowing', or is it more an interpretive grid which has been made available to us as scholars? And in what way does it amount to *knowledge*? What is the rationality, intelligence, mode of connection or communication that produces a contagion in which unknown, unconnected, groups begin to riot as if spontaneously, when all they share appears to be nothing other than loosely equivalent urban and socioeconomic contexts?

These are not questions that we can hope to answer here, for they would require an immense amount of contextualising and analysing. But we can at least sketch out something of the context and then reflect on the relations between media and culture and their implications here. What led to the November 2010 protests in the UK is essentially this. Following a close-run and unclear election in May 2010, which led to a hung parliament, with no clear winner, the UK lost a Labour government and gained a government made up of a coalition of the Conservative Party and the Liberal Democrat Party. This coalition government inherited a budget deficit whose existence they brandished as their warrant to introduce some of the most draconian cuts to public spending ever seen in the UK. The rhetoric was one of necessity, but of course the decision to slash public spending and investment was precisely that: a *decision*, a political decision, one which was evidently weighted by a neoliberal ideological bias. There are always ways of trying to balance something as complex as a national budget other than by making spending cuts. What is at issue here is the fact that cutting back public spending is nothing more nor less than the preferred economic policy of neoliberal thinking that has defined the UK's Conservative party since the rise of Margaret Thatcher in the late 1970s and through the 1980s.

Neoliberalism refers to a type of economic and political thinking which holds that the State is inefficient and the 'free market' should be left to 'correct' inefficiency and inequality. The argument is essentially that humans should be allowed to be 'homo economicus', or rational profit-maximising animals, and that, accordingly, society will profit and prosper. Neoliberal theory is therefore entirely pro-capitalist and hostile to any form of thinking that might be critical of its principles of stringent individualism and (literal) anti-sociality. Neoliberalism often advocates the need for inequality, arguing that there is a 'trickle down' logic to wealth distribution, in which it is beneficial for all that a minority become super-rich, because that massive wealth

(Continued)

will 'trickle down' to many people. According to many cultural, political, historical and economic thinkers, researchers, academics and experts, neoliberal principles are short on evidence of success and have a long track record of amplifying inequality and devastating non-Western economies.

The current stage in the process of the imposed expansion of neoliberalisation in the UK began with the publication of a review of government spending on higher education, called the 'Independent Review of Higher Education Funding and Student Finance', or, more informally, and following the name of the lead investigator, Lord Browne, 'the Browne Review'. This review recommended the removal of government funding for the delivery of all arts, humanities and social science teaching in universities in England, with a move towards full economic costing for the delivery of university education through the introduction of considerably higher fees for students. However, at the same time as making an espousal of market principles, a fundamental lack of faith in these principles was demonstrated: 'core' and 'key' subjects in science, technology, engineering, and mathematics (STEM) would be protected from market mechanisms; these 'STEM' subjects would continue to receive state funding and massive cross-subsidisation. Also, an upper limit or cap was placed on the level of fees universities could charge, so the market would not be 'free' after all. The contradictions here are glaring.

The eponymous Lord Browne, whose name appears on the informal title of the review is a former boss of British Petroleum (BP).[1] Indeed, this is the man who, had he stayed on with BP, would have taken the rap for the Gulf of Mexico BP oil catastrophe (McQuillan 2010a). The most pertinent feature of his legacy is the fact that Lord Browne had always, for the full length of his career, been entirely committed to making spending cuts; so much so that he has been held up as a key contender for the person who arguably ought to be deemed most responsible for the BP disaster in the first place – insofar as it was a disaster fundamentally caused by cost-cutting shortcuts in safety mechanisms. (Browne was also head of BP at the time of the 2005 Texas City oil refinery disaster.) Other authors of the Browne Review included the mastermind of the 2008 UK bailout of the banking system by the UK government, as well as management consultants, employees of McKinsey and people who had close connections with the first titanic failure of a capitalist institution that had been deemed 'too big to fail', ENRON (Dale 2010). Like the Titanic (the ocean-going liner that had been believed to be too huge to sink), ENRON blazed a trail which many other huge capitalist institutions soon followed.

In other words, while the track records of the authors of the Browne Review are not spotless success stories, they are nevertheless impeccable representatives of the dominant or hegemonic economic rationality – that rationality which claims that cutting government intervention or intrusion into markets will free them up to act more efficiently. This is an ideological argument at the heart of neoliberal economic thinking based on a belief about 'the invisible hand'. The problem with it is that this dogma always goes hand in hand with an undeclared heavy-handed legal and State interventionism into more and more regions of society. This interventionism is required in order to produce and to police the behaviour of putatively 'free' markets.[2] In line with this thinking, the Browne Review recommended that billions of pounds be cut, including a 100 per cent reduction in funding for arts, humanities and social sciences.

Unfortunately, this hodgepodge neoliberal thinking overlooked a key dimension of the theoretical and ideological underpinning of right-wing economic theory and ideology since Thatcher: namely, the classical economics of Adam Smith. What is overlooked in the marketisation of education is Adam Smith's acknowledgement, in book five of *The Wealth of Nations*, that education falls into the category of a non-economic institution that *must* nevertheless be funded by the state because the economy can't fund the right sort of education (namely, putatively 'useless' education: arts, humanities and culture), and without an artistic and cultural education society and the economy will fall into a vicious circle of decline and be unable even to provide a workforce, let alone lead the way in a global knowledge economy.

As Robert J. C. Young has pointed out (Young 1992), this ultimately suggests that Adam Smith's belief in the power of the free market to sort itself out is irrational, insofar as Smith's conviction that non-useful (i.e. non-vocational, non-utilitarian) education must be funded by the state (because it has a fundamental and incalculable value) contradicts his entire premises.[3] (As an aside, however, this also suggests that the best thing that any remaining revolutionary Marxists could do now would be to wholeheartedly support all government cuts and all expansions of capitalism, because these cuts and developments could be theoretically regarded as helping to speed up the demise of capitalism.)[4]

Martin McQuillan, the Dean of Arts at Kingston University, called the recommendations of the Browne Review 'the nuclear option': a policy that would lead to the total and irreversible destruction of everything whose target is other than financial. McQuillan represented it all as a death blow for critical thought itself. Writing about similar cuts in Ireland, Graham Allen stated, 'The future has been cancelled' (McQuillan 2010a).

However, these actions had their reactions. In reaction to the government's approbation and proposed implementation of the recommendations in the Browne Review, there were quickly popular cultural reactions, in media, in journalism and on the streets. Marches began in London on 10 November 2010, signalling the beginning of a winter of discontent in the UK. The protests against proposed government cuts in the UK throughout the winter became objects of social and political attention, because of outbreaks of violence and questionable police tactics, specifically the new process of 'kettling' protestors, as discussed earlier.

Playing war games

According to news reports in *The Independent* newspaper in February 2011, in response to the first wave of protests against its cuts, the UK government started to play 'war games'[5]: theoretical computer simulated enactments of various scenarios of how a period of protest, demonstration, striking and political mobilisation may play itself out and be combated, dominated, controlled and defeated by the government. The government, in other words, began to prepare for the civil war of the tumult of mass and widespread protest. It began to do this on the reasonable assumption that its cutting of spending on public services would provoke widespread anger. In other words, cause and response, action and reaction are increasingly carefully planned for; with the ideal being that as little as possible be left to chance.

However, the type of conflict that the government prepared the police and its PR departments for was the traditional confrontational kind of strike action and marching in the streets. It evidently sought to become more prepared to fight this sort of conflict on all fronts: from micrological and technical (how are protests to be policed and managed) to mediatic and political (how are conflicts to be spun in the media and in parliament) to pragmatic (how might they be used to political advantage – for instance, to usher in private companies to provide the services that striking workers are withholding – the very thing that the government ultimately wants, in many cases, in fact) to legislatively (how might protesting and striking actually be criminalised).

The police planned for this because all of this has happened before, and will happen again. And it is something that anyone concerned to act politically must always bear in mind: politics always involves the planning for a political response; and this response relates to responses on the streets, in the media, in parliament, and in the courts. As became clear in 2010–11, any government is likely not only to plan to break strikes but actually to make strikes work for its own ends. However, as also became clear during 2011, protestors and opponents of the government seemed equally capable of playing their own war games, albeit according to different paradigms and scenarios than those envisaged by traditional confrontational protest.

The first case to consider is that of UKuncut. UKuncut was what cultural theorists might call a kind of non-hierarchical, non-identitarian desiring assemblage. That is, it was from the outset an impassioned and *fundamentally technologically mediated* facilitator of movement. It was a Twitter hashtag, a Facebook page, a website, a mailing list, a point of identification, a way of making rallying calls, a place to find words and vocabularies and arguments and accusations and evidence, and facts and figures and calls to arms and suggestions for creative demonstrations of an anti-governmental and anti-cuts message. Crucially, it seems, it was at the same time *its own reporting on and representation of its own and others' activities.* In this way, it arguably represented something quite new and immensely promising.

UKuncut was not necessarily connected to any single or concrete institution, and was animated by a wholehearted anti-cut and anti-injustice ethos. It employed and operated according to non-mainstream and non-standard forms of communication and action: Twitter, Facebook and routes of direct (but technologically mediated) messaging. But at the same time, older political channels remained (and remain) operative. For instance, the many institutions that were actually facing cuts: these acted via their own representatives – basically, their unions. And their unions went on to call for strikes. And these strikes played themselves out through standard narrative structures and tropes and representations and vocabularies: the media spoke of a radical minority and the police blamed strikers and protestors and the protestors blamed the police; and people may or may not sympathise and always soon grow sick of being unable to get or do what the striking workers used to enable them to get or do. In other words, traditional political forms and media forms continued – and will continue – to play key roles: union representatives speak with management representatives and political representatives in a formal and mediatised discourse. This is the terrain on which the 'police' and government war games were planned in 2010–11. The focus was on police management, media management and discursive management. The aim was the domination of these scenes.

But Twitter and UKuncut stood for new and alternative repositories of strategies and tactics. For, during the political antagonisms begun in 2010, workers could only protest their own particular plight via the mechanism of the union *if* a union is present or active. And the presence or absence of formalised protest depends very much on the specific institution or sector. Some cut sectors may be unable to protest through the usual unionised channels. This is where assemblages like UKuncut can come into their own. UKuncut was from the outset a media-driven phenomenon. Its immediate importance related to the way that its energies were directed towards and articulated with 'particular' protests. At the same time as being connected to specific struggles, it was also relentlessly involved in the creative, performative 'exposing' of the financial and ethical misdemeanours of banks and big businesses.

The communication, coordination and mobilisation enabled by technologies like Twitter, in particular actions and occupations, proved to be quite remarkable. Protestors, demonstrators and occupiers communicated with each other, informed each other, boosted each other's morale, at the same time as informing anyone inclined to find out about what is going on, in a way which bypassed or started to overtake the slower temporality, limitations and inevitably biased institutions of mainstream TV, radio, print and even online news media. In other words, the media technology worked as a supplement to politics and to representation – or as a supplement to politics because it changed the logic or regime of representation.

Moreover, this was a politics of creativity and not negativity. It was a kind of direct action, but it was not premised on the defensive negativity of striking. Here, UKuncut picked up the direct action baton of Reclaim the Streets, who in the 1990s would occupy roads and thoroughfares as part of green political demonstration. But UKuncut staged teach-ins about economics and tax avoidance in high street stores, opened libraries and childcare crèches in high street banks and so on. This became a very media savvy, creative and playful approach to politics and protest.

Much of this strategy took the form of what Slavoj Žižek once called a strategy of over-identification. That is to say, such political performances took the literal and explicit words of power at face value and demanded their actualisation. For instance, one frequent strategy involved the following sorts of thinking: so, if Cameron claims to want a 'big society', let's perform *our* interpretation of this, ideally at the same time as clarifying our idea's beautiful difference from the stark ugliness of the institutions that the government supports. Anything that is mobilised along the lines of 'but *you said* you wanted this' is a kind of over-identification, and according to Žižek, it can sometimes be the most effective way of subverting power, the most subversive thing possible, as it reveals the lie or the obscenity or the hypocrisy of those who made the claims in the first place.

This kind of consciousness-raising performance is certainly valuable. In that context and arguably also in today's context, it always seems easy (and urgent and important) to draw and reiterate the stark contrasts which illustrate the obscenity and hypocrisy of the state of affairs. For instance: multimillion and multibillion pound profits and bonuses for the bailed-out banks in the face of unemployment and misery dished out to providers of vital public services. But it need not be the bailed-out bankers of post-2008. One might look at all manner of inegalitarian occurrence in society, such as the pay-rises awarded to many university Vice Chancellors or those at the top of the NHS, and so on, in conjunction with pointing out the drastic cuts the public were told 'we all' had to make, and which mainly took the form of cuts to front-line staff and services. A politics of over-identification in such a situation would say: 'but you said we were all in this together. How come the rich get richer and the poor get poorer?' Or: 'if we are all in this together, how come it is not the case that everyone, everywhere, all the way up and down the chain of an institution, takes equivalent pay and budgetary cuts? If this were *really* about the figures and about the money – about balancing the books – then wouldn't cuts at the very top result in much greater savings than cuts at the bottom?'

In slightly different terms, the philosopher Jacques Rancière notes that there have been great changes in the orientation of political protest since the 1960s. He notes that in the 1960s, protestors tended to be 100 per cent *against* the powerful and their institutions. But this meant that there could be no dialogue: for, on the one hand, the protestors believed that every word said by power was evil; on the other hand, the representatives of institutions believed that the protestors were just silly children who deserved only contempt. But, more recently, Rancière observes, protest has been less millenarian or less based in outright opposition. Protest has been more about contesting particular *clauses*, the *wording* of proposed legislation, complaints about *details*, technicalities, interpretations, and so on. Rancière calls this a politics of verification.

UKuncut lead the way in a certain new-media-led performative politics of over-identification. It was organised by an argumentative or rhetorical politics of verification. It was not a party politics. And perhaps is raises more questions than it answers. But what is clear is that the new media politics of performance and verification has bypassed old media, has multiplied the accessibility of representations, and has started to subvert older institutions and authorities. The question is, how much can it change? 'Institutions' run deep, and, as the next chapter seeks to illustrate, mediation and media representation arguably has profound effects on all levels of culture, right down to the production and reproduction of the most intimately felt senses of identity.

4 Filming Culture

Post-cinematic effects

The 19th Century was arguably the century of the dominance of literature and of the British Empire. Literature was the dominant cultural form; Britain the dominant national force. To the extent that this is the case, then it can also be said that the 20th Century was the century of the United States of America and cinema. The USA emerged as the dominant (or hegemonic) cultural and economic force and presence, with the cinema as the dominant cultural form or technology. The complex processes involved are often distilled into the word 'Hollywood', a term which evokes the global ideological hold of the USA and the channelling of that ideology through the film form and the cinematic apparatus.

What then, is the 21st Century? Historians of all areas of life – from culture to economics, from military to market, from language to technology – have proposed that the 21st Century seems likely to be the century of China and the Internet. We will have to defer a serious consideration of the question of 'China', here – although it is fascinating (Chow 1993; Park 2010) – and begin from the question: what kind of cultural form or technology is the Internet? As I write these words in 2011 the jury is still out. Rather than trying to predict the future by trying to anticipate the cultural significance and development of the internet, let us first consider the fate of the older 20th Century cultural technology of film in the context of the emergence of the internet.

Some cultural theorists have recently started talking of the transition from a *cinematic* age to a *post-cinematic* age. Such an idea will doubtless undergo further revision and elaboration and find a much more precise formulation as time goes on. But for now, Steven Shaviro's *Post-Cinematic Affect* (Shaviro 2010) leads the way in this regard, by engaging with the effects of post-cinematic technologies on our experiences, orientations, emotions, feelings and lives.

'Post-cinematic' technologies include all that is associated with the rise of interactivity, gaming, multimedia and the proliferation of different Internet platforms, as well as various new types of text, such as the music video, the new ways, modes and contexts of experiencing and consuming them and the effects they have on consciousness and perception. Shaviro considers the rise to dominance of these 'post-cinematic' technologies in terms of a transformation of 'affects': mutations of experiential landscapes, emotional geographies, and perceptual and sensorial ecosystems. Using a famous term developed by the pioneer of cultural studies, Raymond Williams (yet developing this term in ways informed by the French philosopher Gilles Deleuze), Shaviro characterises this as an epochal transformation in dominant 'structures of feeling'. In other words, the rise of the post-cinematic context has transformed our lives in ways related to our day-to-day and moment-to-moment experience.

If such post-cinematic technologies have transformed structures of feeling, this is not the first time this has happened. For instance, we might consider the emergence of cinema itself. Rey Chow opens her 1995 book *Primitive Passions* (1995) with a reconsideration of the famous story of the turn towards a writing career of the monumental figure of Chinese literature, Lu Xun. While he was a medical student at the very beginning of the 20th Century, Lu Xun watched with horror the cinema newsreels depicting atrocities committed in the Russo-Japanese War in Manchuria, including the executions of Chinese people. Lu Xun's account of his response to these sights is complex and provocative. Indeed, his response to these first cinematic newsreels actually prefigure many of the dominant questions that have arisen in the face of cinema and other forms of viewing or 'passive consumption' of mass media messages. For instance, Lu Xun asked, how could the witnesses to executions be so *passive*; how could audiences, of any kind, *do nothing*; and, more to the point, what could he himself do here and now, to address such wrongs and escape the incapacity and passivity of being nothing but a viewer?

These first problems, arising very early on in response to the first cinematic experiences of news reports, arguably set out many of the entrenched problems associated with the cinema, especially the problem of a sense of incapacity, castration, helplessness and passivity. Rey Chow's analysis of Lu Xun's emotional and intellectual response is far reaching and immensely important (Chow 1995). But the ultimate point I want to single out and draw attention to here is one that Chow emphasises about the significance of the fact that this new technology (the *cinematic* apparatus) precipitated a peculiar response from Lu Xun: he turned away from his chosen career path of medicine and towards *literature*, believing that he could do more to improve the health of China by cultural (or ideological) intervention than by medical intervention.

Central to Chow's reading of this famous narrative is the following: Xun's response to the new cultural technology (cinema) sends him into a relationship with an *older* technology (literature). From this, Chow proposes that it is possible to perceive the effects of *cinema* in (and on) Xun's *literature*. From this point, one may broaden the perspective and begin to grasp the significance of the emergence of *cinema* in much, if not all, subsequent developments in *literature*. Indeed, we might even be tempted to regard the majority of 20th-Century literature as 'post-cinematic', in that it is literature produced in a cultural world that the cinematic apparatus has intervened into, dominated and transformed.

In other words, after the birth of cinema, literature could never be the same again. In this sense, Lu Xun's story is exemplary of the epochal mutation entailed in the shocks of modernity. Literature in modernity is itself post-cinematic, even if this reverses the chronological periodisation and emphasis that organises Shaviro's book. For, the 'post-cinematic' that Shaviro refers us to is of course all that new stuff that comes *after* cinema: computers, the Internet, the dynamism and interactivity of gaming or web 2.0; before that, cable and satellite TV, multiple (indeed myriad) television and radio channels, video, DVD and all the rest. Nevertheless, as was implicit even in the very first theorisations of the word 'postmodern' by such philosophers as Jean-François Lyotard, one of the key points about the postmodern is that everything you can say about the features of the 'post' are actually already there, at the outset, before the emergence of the period of 'the post' as such (Lyotard 1984): so you can see elements of post-modernity at the origins (and throughout) the historical period called modernity. Postmodern thinkers such as Lyotard have long pointed out that the postmodern is implied in and active in the very emergence of the modern, right from the start.

Rey Chow's reading of Lu Xun's affective response to these early experiences of (or encounters with) cinema demonstrates this explicitly. The new technology intervenes into, informs and thereby transforms the cultural landscape in ways which have knock on (albeit unpredictable) effects on other forms of cultural production and reception. To see this at a basic level, one need merely consider the extent to which so many literary best-sellers today have clearly been written with the production requirements of the standard Hollywood film form firmly in mind. This is but one register of the hegemony or dominance of the cinematic form and its 'hegemonisation' even of other cultural realms, such as literature.

In any case, Steven Shaviro argues that contemporary cultural conditions are such that that the cinematic epoch is coming to a close. We are now at the end(s) of the cinematic. This is being registered *within* cinema, even though cinema remains strongly influential across all of its inheritors – all of the new technologies that are taking cinematic technologies forward in new directions. This is why the times are to be regarded as 'post-cinematic' and not 'anti' or 'non-cinematic'. Cinema is on the wane while other technological forms are on the rise, just as the USA is on the wane in terms of its global hegemony, while China is on the rise in terms of economic and military strength. Thus, gaming, all things interactive, the music video and other new arrivals on the audiovisual technological scene all remain hugely informed by cinematography, but they move away from its technological limitations.

Meanwhile, cinema attempts to incorporate the new technological advancements within itself: from DVD menus, extras, commentaries, outtakes, integrated marketing strategies with other realms (gaming, animation, toys and merchandise and spin-off series) and other supplements, all the way to the inclusion of forms of interactivity that ultimately signal the demise of the older form. According to this perspective, films like *Blade Runner* (1982, Dir Ridley Scott) or *S1m0ne* (2002, Dir Andrew Nichol) are not post-cinematic, while *The Matrix* (1999, Dir Larry and Andy Wachowski) or even the Korean film *Old Boy* (2003, Dir Chan-wook Park) are. The former are films *about* future technologies, while the latter *incorporate* future technologies into themselves, insofar as both films famously affect the styles of computer simulated choreographies in their most famous fight scenes, albeit in different ways: *The Matrix* employs the sharpness and precision of arcade game fights, while *Old Boy* incorporates the two-dimensional plane of older forms of computer game, but it counterbalances this with the inclusion of all of the scrappiness, imprecision, stumbling, gasping, moaning and indeed, *messy brawling* that almost all action films exclude or repress (as exemplified by the ultra-precise choreography of *The Matrix* or *The Bourne Identity* trilogy (2002, Dir Doug Liman; 2004 Dir Paul Greengrass; 2007, Dir Paul Greengrass)).

Classic cinematic effects

Now, whether post-cinematic or classically cinematic, one important question is that of what the cinema *does*, or what the cinematic apparatus *does*: what effects this type of media has on people, what difference it makes to culture and society. As already mentioned, one abiding argument made especially by Marxist thinkers is that the cinema makes us *passive* (Adorno and Horkheimer 1986). As we saw in the previous chapters, some thinkers have been concerned that societies dominated primarily by the imposition of viewing relations, in which we're all spectators, not only make us passive but actually make us acquiescent to or even enthusiastic for the worst kinds of political power. In the worst cases we can become enthusiastic for populist or fascist dictators who exploit the cinematic apparatus to make us think that they are charismatic, wise, authoritative, avuncular or loveable father figures or suchlike. At the very least, it is clear that we can have our heart-strings plucked by formulaic and clichéd devices of emotional or affective manipulation.

The cover of Guy Debord's classic, *The Society of the Spectacle* – one of the most influentially pessimistic Marxist texts about the effects of a media saturated society – has an image of rows of transfixed viewers sitting in a cinema, all facing towards the screen, all equally and identically enthralled. This has become one of the defining images of the positions which see a media saturated society as one which produces passivity, not only in audiences but effectively in everyone. (Debord 1994)

But this argument about passivity, docility or plasticity is not the end of the story about cinematic effects. One of the most influential analyses of the ideological effects of the cinematic apparatus was set out by Laura Mulvey in 1975. In an essay titled 'Visual Pleasure and Narrative Cinema' (Mulvey 1975), Mulvey uses psychoanalytic (and not Marxist) theory to argue that 'the unconscious of patriarchal society has structured film form'. Specifically, she argues, the regular repeated 'image of the castrated woman [is used by Hollywood film] to give order and meaning to its world'. The men fight for the woman. They fight over the woman. The drama circles around the woman. So, 'woman' is 'tied to her place as bearer of meaning', but she is not the 'maker of meaning'. The woman is objectified. She is the motive force of the action, but she is essentially excluded from it.

Specifically, argues Mulvey, in classic Hollywood, woman is the object of the gaze. She is there *to be looked at*. And this has significant implications, she argues. For it clarifies the extent to which filmic and other media images work to reinforce patriarchal, sexist or misogynistic ideologies.

A clear example of what Mulvey calls the classic effect of such a style can be seen in many pop music videos. Perhaps the best, to my knowledge, is that of the video for the song 'Ayo Technology', performed by Justin Timberlake and Fifty Cent. In this video, set in London, we see the male performers play ersatz James Bond characters. However, although they are slick-suited and sporting various forms of weaponry and technological gadgets, like Bond, they are not spying on villains, criminals, terrorists, or other stock kinds of anti-hero; rather they are spying on various female characters. Early shots in the video see them looking through night-vision goggles and peering through the sights of large guns at women who are scantily clad and, in unusual locations, performing strangely incongruous erotic dances. An early moment sees Fifty Cent spying through a gunsight from a rooftop, looking down at a girl dressed only in her underwear and high heels as she gets into a sports car.

Other scenes see Timberlake spying through binoculars from a chauffeur-driven car at a woman who is writhing in underwear, back-lit, in silhouette, in the window of a city flat or apartment. Later on in the video, Timberlake and Fifty Cent also appear to command futuristic sci-fi-like technologies, which can evidently act on women at a distance: Fifty Cent controls a virtual computer akin to the device that Tom Cruise uses to see events with omniscience in *Minority Report* (2002, Dir Steven Spielberg). For Tom Cruise's police officer character in the movie, the computer functions to help him master imponderable amounts of data and to perform calculations that attempt to predict the future. Fifty Cent, however, uses a similar-looking device in such a way as to make women become sexually aroused.

Eventually, the video devolves down to the protagonists entering a private or luxury and exclusive lap-dancing club. This has all the hallmarks of a traditional upper-class London 'gentleman's club', plus strippers. At this point, we see the male protagonists enjoy lap-dances while being blindfolded, as if inverting the original form of pleasure:

at the start of the video, the men enjoy the scopophilia of looking and desiring. By the end, in contrast to the common understanding of the etiquette of lap-dancing establishments, in which customers can typically look but not touch, the males, in being blindfolded, are evidently now allowed to touch. Apparently, being blindfold will enhance this experience for them. (This scene is intercut with other scenes in which Timberlake also appears elsewhere: erotic scenes on the stairways, in the doorways and on the landings of a residential apartment building.)

There is much that could be said about such a video, and many others like it. From the perspective offered by Laura Mulvey, the video first illustrates the desiring, objectifying and controlling aspirations of *the male gaze*. The male gaze is a voyeuristic, 'scopophilic', controlling gaze, she argues. It is a sexualised and sexualising gaze. It literally *targets* the female form and objectifies it. In this case, the gunsight through which Fifty Cent spies is clearly a phallic image. The gun targets the woman, and the act of sighting the women is in itself an enactment of power. He could easily 'shoot'. He could easily 'take' her. He feels in control. The decision is in his hands. In a sense, therefore, he is already in control, by virtue of his viewing position.

Similarly, the night-vision binoculars used by Timberlake confer upon the screen the green tint that has been associated (in film and television, in news, fact and fiction) not only with security cameras and military weapons but also with the visual look of various much publicised celebrities' private/personal pornographic sex tapes. Many of these came to light at around the same time as this music video. The Paris Hilton sex tapes are perhaps the most famous (and perhaps most cruel) example of videos which emerged around that time. Moreover, at these points, the camera angle changes to that of a hand-held private or amateur video, which emphasises the pornographic allusions. (This song, 'Ayo Technology', was reputedly first titled 'Ayo Pornography', but the decision was taken to rename it and change the lyrics accordingly because the word 'pornography' would damage its ability to receive prime time TV and radio airplay, and hence maximise sales and revenues.)

So, the video performs a certain male fantasy of desire, control and sexualising objectification. At the same time as this, and in a way that is entirely consistent with Mulvey's argument, the video depicts women as reciprocally (or perhaps even primarily) performing for a male gaze – and, crucially, even when a literal male gaze is not normally assumed to be present. The case of the female figure writhing at the window is the clearest example. For, via this scenario, the video seems to suggest, this is precisely the way that beautiful women will behave when they undress; that even when they believe themselves to be home alone and are changing their clothes, they are still basically 'asking for it'.

The idea of identity as 'performance' – that is, as something that is not simply natural or inevitable, but is rather a culturally obligatory performance – was perhaps most popularized in the arguments of the early work of Judith Butler. It has since become widely accepted in cultural and media studies (as well as the humanities more widely), and it has significant implications for what we might call the politics of media and culture – for part of the argument is that we learn how to 'perform', how to 'be', from what we *see*.

There are many implications and ramifications here. The video reiterates a version of masculinity as gaze and femininity as 'to-be-looked-at-ness' – or male as controlling and female as controlled. With the lyrical repetition of 'oh, she wants it, oh, I'm gonna give it to her', and similar sentiments, it repeats the misogynistic perspective that women are 'asking for it'. But, the question then becomes one of our agencies in front of the text. Or in other words: once we see that the text is patriarchal, misogynistic and sexist, the question is, does that mean that the viewer will be or become patriarchal, misogynistic and sexist? Is the viewer *passive*? Does the filmic text manipulate us the way that the virtual technology used by Fifty Cent in the video manipulates the woman?

I am reluctant to propose that the watching of videos, films, TV or other media is going to generate a case of 'monkey see, monkey do'. In other words, I am not proposing that such videos in and of themselves cause or deepen misogyny or patriarchy. However, this is certainly a possibility that needs to be entertained. For, according to the implications of Mulvey's approach, what such texts do is that they *normalise* these patriarchal viewing relations: we – male and female – become *used to* (habituated, acclimatised) viewing the world this way, to apprehending the female as body, as object, as sex, and to regarding the male as powerful, controlling, gazing; we get used to regarding the woman as *wanting* to masquerade and 'perform' her femininity as her sexuality for the male gaze and so on.

Another clear example of this can be seen in many Beyoncé songs and videos, in which apparently 'feminist' sentiments are uttered – declarations about 'independence' and 'strength', for instance, which might, at first glance seem to be feminist. But the problem is that these sentiments emerge within songs which are otherwise entirely organised by the performance of desire for a man. One song, which claims to celebrate strong independent femininity, nevertheless repeats the phrase 'if you like[d] it then you should have put a ring on it'. In other words, the song is organised by a kind of bitterness – a bitterness about and a desire for male commitment. Such resentment hardly seems to be a feminist sentiment, or even the sentiment of a truly 'free' and 'independent' person. Rather, in this performance, we see a combination of contradictory sentiments which show that the celebration of independence is in fact a grudging resentful response to the disappointment elicited when the (absent) male refused to 'put a ring on it' – that is, to commit, to get engaged or married. To this extent, all the words about 'feminism' or 'strength' in the song are a mere replaying of the most patriarchal of assumptions or stereotypes about males and females: that men will not commit, and that all women really want is a man.

Many other of Beyoncé's 'feminist' or 'post-feminist' songs replay this logic: the character who frantically performs her desire through myriad costume changes and insanely energetic erotic performances in front of an entirely stationary and unresponsive 'cool' male character; or the woman who ditches her partner because he is not up to scratch, singing about how she will be 'over you in a minute' and that she will have 'another [one of] you in a minute' – all of which confirm that ultimately what is desired is standard patriarchal heterosexual domesticity.

But just because these popular cultural media texts are evidently patriarchal, sexist and *heteronormative* (in that they reiterate the message that heterosexual norms are both the standard and the objective), does this mean *either* that we are passive before such texts *or* that we ourselves will 'become' patriarchal, sexist and heteronormative ourselves by virtue of our exposure to them?

There are many approaches to culture and identity which propose that we may 'become' what we are exposed to. However, many of these are simplistic (or indeed what is termed 'essentialist'), in that they propose that we will essentially 'become' what we are exposed to, and particularly perhaps what we enjoy. And, it is important to note, we may well enjoy Beyoncé's or Timberlake's videos, and for any number of reasons: we may find the beat irresistible; we may be enthralled by the faces and bodies in the videos; or the sheer complexity and rapidity of the flashing and changing scenes in a music video may be compelling. But does our enjoyment make us a prisoner or a puppet? The situation is surely more complex.

The cultural critic bell hooks once provided an interesting account of the problems of rap, hip hop music and black youth identity in the 1980s and early 1990s. Hip hop was arguably one of the main contexts in which black youth culture gained anything like cultural visibility and prominence. During the 1990s and up to the early 2000s, hip hop and rap could actually be said to have utterly transformed mainstream popular music and global popular culture in myriad ways. But there was a problem at the heart of it. According to hooks, the black rapper *character* and the hip hop music video *style* became entangled with a damaging image of blackness.

The logic, according to hooks, is that of a vicious circle. The circle is this: first, hip hop gains prominence as a black musical genre. It is associated with poor black youth and also with anger and protest. It is organised by a connection with 'the street'. This all gives hip hop and rap a strong identity. But it also becomes a cliché, a stereotype, a cheap commodity. It becomes another way of defining the black: angry, dangerous, poor, politicised, apparently aggressive and often violent. Over time, sexuality comes to the fore too. Black rap and hip hop videos (along with white spin offs and related enterprises) increasingly involve the tried and tested marketing device of always including sexy female 'eye candy'. So what becomes produced is *a genre which can all too easily act as a stand in for black culture per se*. This genre – and this interpretation of what black culture is – becomes reduced to violence, guns, money and girls.

Now, what hooks proposes is not that 'people' (viewers, listeners) simply 'change' and 'become' more violent or more sexist. Rather, it is that certain generic and formulaic rules, sorts of lyrics, types of imagery and styles of video (involving guns, girls and money) gains a dominance and acts as a kind of stranglehold. To be a success, artists perceive that the easy – or the only – route is to produce texts and performances that now conform to this new norm. In other words, what Adorno and Horkheimer called *the culture industry* produces cultural and media effects, effects which play themselves out in people's daily lives, fantasies and desires.

Because of the complexity of this relation between personal identity, media, institutions, discourses and their effects, let us conclude this section with a consideration of the complexity of the interplay of media and culture, identity and ethnicity, as can be seen from an analysis of merely one possible media/cultural text. Many others could have been chosen. This one has been selected because it prompts us to think about so many things, themes and areas of our own lives, 'fantasies' and relationships with media and cultural images.

Media culture and coercive mimeticism

The music video for the song 'Pretty Fly for a White Guy' (Offspring 1998) is instructive in this regard. In the music video, the words 'all the girlies say I'm pretty fly for a white guy' are uttered by a stereotypical white 'wannabe'. The lyrics narrate the tale – or rather, the situation – the plight – of an apparently affluent, suburban white American teenager who fetishises and fantasises about edgy non-white ethnicity. In the video, we see several of the scenarios which define his phantasy. Whether black African-American or Latino, our eponymous 'white guy' wannabe wants-to-be *that*: he identifies *with*, he fantasises *as* that. He wants to be one of *them*. Unfortunately, what is absolutely clear here is that the one thing he is not is 'pretty fly'. Rather, he is presented as ridiculous, a fool, utterly lacking in self-awareness or self-knowledge – living, as the lyrics put it, 'in denial'.

So, the song is all about getting it wrong, wanting the impossible and denying that impossibility. The reason for wanting the impossible boils down to a phantasy.[1] This is dramatised in the call-and-response (and commentary) that opens and permeates the song. The song opens with it: a female chorus chant 'Give it to me baby'. In the video, our hapless hero responds in the affirmative. This call and response is repeated. It is a chant of female call and male response that dramatises what is evidently a male sexual phantasy about specifically ethnic female desire. It is followed by the gravelly-voiced claim: 'And all the girlies say I'm pretty fly for a white guy', whereupon the song 'proper' begins. This, it soon becomes clear, is the structuring fantasy of our misrecognising, fantasising white guy. This is what he wants. This is what he thinks it would be like if only he were the ethnic he wants to be. This is what he wants to see and hear. He imagines the call. He 'performs' (as they say) a response. So, in the video representation, the song runs: repeated female chant ('Give it to me baby'); he answers ('uh huh, uh huh'). This is followed by the voice of his phantasy, which asserts his conviction that 'all the girlies say I'm pretty fly for a white guy'.

After this intro, we are 'counted-in' in incorrect Spanish ('Uno, dos, tres, cuatro, cinco, cinco, seis'). If we had been in any doubt up until now, this *miscount* – this moment of getting it just a bit but fundamentally wrong – not quite getting the Spanish right – clarifies things for us. This is a joke. This is about misrecognition, getting it wrong. Moreover, the girls in the video are clearly non-existent fantasy constructions: there never were girls thronging around him on the way to his car, by the side of the road, or covered in glittering paint by the pool. They are entirely his phantasy.

An initial assessment of the song, taking into account any mirth it might produce – and the extent to which we might share, understand or 'get' the joke – suggests that this popular cultural text is saying something quite precise about identity, 'cultural' identity, 'identity performativity' and ethnicity. And this appears to be something quite different from what is widely supposed to be held by many thinkers, from Judith Butler to Homi Bhabha and beyond. For, the text is saying at least one, or perhaps all, of the following: (1) that a white ethnic cannot – or should not – try to 'perform' another ethnic identity; (2) that trying to be other than white for the white is ridiculous; (3) that trying to do or to be so is premised on 'not getting it', on 'denial'; (4) that white ethnicity is not like other ethnicities – not porous, not dilutable, not 'hybridisable' or 'fragile'; and (5) that the only compensation for the sadness and disappointment that this might cause for our wannabe is the contemporary Confessional: 'At least you know you can always go on Ricki Lake'. Indeed, don't worry, be happy, add The Offspring: 'the world needs wannabes'. So, 'hey, hey, do the brand new thing'.

The song is very clear on this. After staging the fantasy scenario, after being miscounted-in, the narrative voice begins to tell us all about it. The lyrics begin by addressing us in terms of a shared lot, a common problem that we all recognise: 'You know it's kinda hard just to get along today'. *We all know this*, right? Furthermore: 'Our subject isn't cool, but he thinks it anyway'. Isn't this a familiar story? How many of us are guilty of it ourselves? We may recall Lacan's contention that, in love, '*You never look at me from the place from which I see you*. Conversely, *what I look at is never what I wish to see*' (Lacan qtd in Chow 1998: 81). Moreover, as Rey Chow points out, this 'dialectic of eye and gaze' need not be *literally* inter-subjective; a man may fall 'in love, not with a woman or even with another man, not with a human being at all but with a thing, a reified form of his own fantasy' (1998: 78). As The Offspring put it: 'He may not have a clue, and he may not have style/But everything he lacks, well he makes up in denial'.

Is *this* his problem: 'denial'? 'Denial' is surely the most abused, misused, bandied-about psychobabblistic term ever. Everyone, it seems risks living in denial. Overcoming denial is indeed an abiding concern of an enormous range of popular cultural texts and discourses. But, if denial is deemed to be the problem, what is deemed to be the solution? The popular answer is come to terms, recognise and accept. But how? By talking about yourself; by *confessing*. Go on Ricki Lake. Even if you are 'fake', you *can* have a moment of real-world, recognised, 'authentic' success ('fame'), by coming clean, by confessing, publicly: the only authentic redemption in a world which thrives on the production of fakes and wannabes, say The Offspring.

If we can laugh at all of this it is also because we can recognise all of this. According to the implications of the argument of Michel Foucault in *The History of Sexuality, Volume 1* (Foucault 1978), this familiarity and recognisability comes from the fact that The Offspring song plays with the material thrown up by and circulating in and as a discursive constellation – a very old discursive constellation, says Foucault, which came together in the 18th Century. In this discursive formation, the terms ethnicity, identity, authenticity and autobiography – or confession – encounter each other in an over-determined chiasmus. In it, whenever issues of identity and ethnicity arise as a (self-reflexive, 'personal') problem, this discursive constellation proposes that the route out is via the self-reflexive side-door of autobiographical (self) confession.

There is more to this than observing that engaging with ethnicity requires an engagement with one's own identity, one that ought to lead into a searching self-interrogation and ideally a deconstruction of questions of authenticity and autobiography – although this is certainly a part of it. For the Foucauldian point is that precisely such discourses of the self, especially in terms of the brands of self-referentiality that nowadays feed chat shows like Ricki Lake, can be seen to have emerged decisively in modernity. And they emerged with an attending argument about self-referentiality's subversive relation to power and its emancipatory relation to truth. That is, it refers us to the implications of Foucault's argument about what he called 'the repressive hypothesis' – namely, that almost irresistible belief that power tries to silence us and demands our silence (Foucault 1978: 18; Chow 2002: 114). As Foucault argued, however, almost the exact opposite is the case. Or rather, even if there are places where power demands silence or discipline, these are more than matched by an exponential explosion and proliferation of discourses – in this case, about the self.

These discourses include arguments about self-referentiality's subversive relation to power and its emancipatory relation to truth, which relates to the Enlightenment idea that an introspective turn to the self is emancipatory: the ingrained idea (whose prehistory is the Catholic Confessional, and whose contemporary ministers Foucault finds in the psychiatrist and psychoanalyst) that seeking to speak the truth of oneself is the best method of getting at our essential truth *and* the best way to resist power. Similarly, modern literary self-referentiality emerged with an attending discourse of resistance – a discourse which regarded *literature 'as such'* as resistance to the instrumentalisation of technical and bureaucratic language, first and foremost. And, by the same token, self-referentiality emerged as an apparently ideal solution to the knotty problem of representing others. For, how do you represent others truthfully, adequately, ethically? The answer here is: you don't. They should represent themselves. Here, the self-reflexivity of self-referentiality is regarded not as apartheid but as *the* way to bypass the problems of representing others – by throwing the option open for everyone to speak the truth of themselves. However, in Foucault's phrase: 'the "Enlightenment", which discovered the liberties, also invented the disciplines' (Foucault 1977: 222; see also Chow 2002: 113). In other words, the desire to refer to the self, to discuss the self, to produce the self discursively, the impulse to autobiography and confession, can be regarded as a consequence of disciplinarity. Psychiatry demands that we reveal our selves. As does psychoanalysis, as do ethnographic focus groups, as do corporate marketing focus groups, not to mention the Confessional, the criminologist and Ricki Lake. And so on. Autobiography and confession are only resistance if power truly tries to repress the production of discourse. Which it doesn't – at least not everywhere.

The point is, autobiography and confession are genealogically wedded – if not welded – to recognisable disciplinary protocols and – perhaps most significantly – proceed according to the terms of recognisable metanarratives. Thus, says Chow:

> When minority individuals think that, by referring to themselves, they are liberating themselves from the powers that subordinate them, they may actually be allowing such powers to work in the most intimate fashion – from within their hearts and souls, in a kind of voluntary surrender that is, in the end, fully complicit with the guilty verdict that has been declared on them socially long before they speak.
>
> (Chow 2002: 115)

‸se, in thinking about postcoloniality, ethnicity, social semiotics
‸ral politics, it is very difficult *not* to think about oneself.

Indeed, even in full knowledge of Foucault, there remains something of a complex *imperative* to do so, even (perhaps especially) if, like me, one does not have a blatantly postcolonial ethnicity in the classic sense – even if, that is, like me, one has an entirely hegemonic socio-cultural identity: an ethnicity without ethnicity, as it were; the *hegemon* of a hegemony; that is, the 'norm'. For, surely one must factor one-self into whatever picture one is painting, in terms of the 'institutional investments that shape [our own] enunciation' (Chow 1993, 2). Indeed, suggests Chow:

the most difficult questions surrounding the demarcation of bound-aries implied by 'seeing' have to do not with positivistic taxonomic juxtapositions of self-contained identities and traditions in the man-ner of 'this is you' and 'that is us', but rather, who is 'seeing' whom, and how? What are the power relationships between the 'subject' and 'object' of the culturally overdetermined 'eye'?

(Chow 1991: 3)

Might acknowledging as much make me pretty fly for a white guy? As thinkers like Robyn Wiegman and Rey Chow have pointed out:

the white subject who nowadays endeavors to compensate for the historical 'wrong' of being white by taking on politically correct agen-das (such as desegregation) and thus distancing himself from his own ethnic history, is seldom if ever accused of being disloyal to his culture; more often than not, he tends to be applauded for being politically progressive and morally superior.

(Chow 2002: 116–117)

Chow proposes that we compare and contrast this with non-white eth-nic subjects – or rather, in her discussion, with non-white ethnic critics, scholars and academics. These subjects, she argues are pressured directly and indirectly to behave 'properly' – to act and think and 'be' the way 'they' are supposed to act and think and be, *as* non-white ethnic aca-demic subjects. If they forget their ethnicity, or their nationalistically or geographically – and hence essentialistically and positivistically – defined 'cultures' and 'heritages', such subjects are deemed to be sell-outs, traitors – *inauthentic*. But, says Chow, if such an ethnic scholar 'should [...] choose, instead, to mimic and perform her own ethnicity' – that is, to respond or perform in terms of the implicit and explicit hail-ing or interpellation of her as an ethnic subject as such, by playing along with the 'mimetic enactment of the automatised stereotypes that are dangled out there in public, hailing the ethnic' (110) – 'she would still be considered a turncoat, this time because she is too eagerly pandering to the orientalist tastes of Westerners' (117), and this time most likely by other non-white ethnic subjects.

Thus, the ethnic subject seems damned if she does and damned if she doesn't 'be' an ethnic subject. Of course, this damnation comes from different parties, and with different implications. But, in any eventuality, Chow's point is that, in sharp contradistinction, 'however far he chooses to go, a white person sympathetic to or identifying with a non-white culture does not in any way become less white' (117). Indeed, she claims:

> When it comes to non-white peoples doing exactly the same thing [...] – that is, becoming sympathetic to or identified with cultures other than their own – we get a drastically different kind of evalua-tion. If an ethnic critic should simply ignore her own ethnic history and become immersed in white culture, she would, needless to say, be deemed a turncoat (one that forgets her origins).
>
> (2002: 117)

It is important to be aware that it is not just whites who pressure the non-white ethnic to conform. Chow gives many examples of the ways that scholars of Chinese culture and literature, for instance, relentlessly produce an essentialist notion of China which is used to berate mod-ern diasporic Chinese (and their cultural productions). This essentialism is an essence that none can live up to, precisely because *they are alive* and as such contaminated, diluted, tainted or corrupted by non-Chinese influences.

At least one side of this key difference between the white and the non-white is dramatised in the Offspring song. While postcolonial crit-ics often recount cases in which non-white ethnic subjects are pressured directly and indirectly to start to behave 'properly' – to act and think and be the way 'they' are supposed to act and think and be as non-white ethnic subjects – in other words, to be both *interpellated*, in Althusser's sense, and *disciplined*, in Foucault's sense – I think that the very intelligi-bility of the Offspring song and its fairly unequivocal condemnation of the white-wannabe-non-white suggests that the white guy who shows too much interest in non-white culture, rather than being 'applauded for being politically progressive and morally superior', can quite easily and will quite frequently be deemed not only 'disloyal to his culture' but ridiculous. *Yet, he remains no less white.* In fact, it seems, *he can become no less white.* But he is still a traitor. Thus, corroborating Chow's thesis, white ethnicity is here presented as absolutely immovable and essentially (or wholly/holy) incorruptible.

Rey Chow calls this 'coercive mimeticism' (2002: 107). Coercive mimeticism designates the way in which the interpellating, disciplining forces of all different kinds of discourses and institutions *call* us into place, *tell* us our place and work to *keep* us in our place. As Chow writes of the ethnic academic subject: 'Her only viable option seems to be that of reproducing a specific version of herself – and her ethnicity – that has, somehow, already been endorsed and approved by the specialists of her culture' (117). Accordingly, coercive mimeticism ultimately works as 'an institutionalised mechanism of knowledge production and dissemination, the point of which is to manage a non-Western ethnicity through the disciplinary promulgation of the supposed difference' (117). As we see through the Offspring song, this disciplinary mechanism extends far beyond the disciplines proper, far beyond the university. In Chow's words:

> unlike the white man, who does not have to worry about impairing his identity even when he is touched by a foreign culture, the ethnic must work hard to keep hers; yet the harder she works at being bona fide, the more of an inferior representation she will appear to be. (124)

Reciprocally, we might add, the harder the white guy tries to be non-white, the 'more' white he will appear. In trying to be other – so say the interpellating voices, tropes, discourses and institutions – he is of course, just being *silly*. Whether this means that the white attempt to be like the other is silly, or that the other is silly – or both – is debatable. What is not debatable is that in all cases 'authenticity' ultimately translates as a hypothetical state of non-self-conscious and non-constructed essential 'being'. The fact that this is an essentialism that is essentially impossible does not mean that it does not 'happen'; rather it means that 'ethnicity' becomes an infinitely supple rhetorical tool. It is available (to anyone and everyone) as a way to disparage both *anyone who is not being the way they are supposed to be* and anyone who *is* being the way they *are* supposed to be.

As Chow explains, 'ethnicity can be used as a means of attacking others, of shaming, belittling, and reducing them to the condition of inauthenticity, disloyalty, and deceit' (124). Ironically, such attacks are 'frequently issued by ethnics themselves against fellow ethnics, that is, the people who are closest to, who are most *like* them ethnically in this fraught trajectory of coercive mimeticism' (124). What this means is that the most contempt, from all quarters, will always be reserved for he or she who does not stay in their place, play their proper ethnicity. All too often, criticism is levelled *individually*, as if it is a *personal* issue, 'despite the fact that this historically charged, alienating situation is a collectively experienced one' (124). Such is the disciplining, streaming, classifying force of coercive mimeticism. Such are the 'uses of ethnicity'.

In the words of Etienne Balibar: 'the problem is to keep "in their place", from generation to generation, those who have no fixed place; and for this, it is necessary that they have a genealogy' (Balibar qtd. in Chow 2002: 95). As such, even the work of sensitive, caring, deeply invested specialists and expert ethnic scholars – even ethnic experts in ethnicity – themselves can function to reinforce ethnicised hierarchies, structured in dominance, simply by insisting on producing their field or object in its difference.

What is at stake here is the surely significant fact that even the honest and principled or declared aim of studying others otherwise can actually amount to a positive working for the very forces one avowedly opposes or seeks to resist. Chow clarifies this in terms of considering the *uncanny proximity but absolute difference* between the disciplinary orientations of cultural studies and area studies. Area studies is a disciplinary field which 'has long been producing "specialists" who report to North American political and civil arenas about "other" civilisations, "other" regimes, "other" ways of life, and so forth' (Chow 1998: 6). However, quite unlike the declared aims and affiliative interests of cultural studies and postcolonial studies in alterity and 'other cultures', within-area studies 'others' are 'defined by way of particular geographical areas and nation states, such as South Asia, the Middle East, East Asia, Latin America and countries of Africa' and are studied as if potential threats, challenges and – hence – ultimately 'information target fields' (6).[2]

Thus, says Chow, there is 'a major difference' between cultural studies and area studies – and indeed between cultural studies and 'normal' academic disciplines per se (Chow 1998: 6–7). This difference boils down to a paradigmatic decision. This is the resistance to 'proper' disciplinarity precisely because of its disciplining effects; the resistance to becoming 'normal' or 'normalised', wherever this might equal allowing power inequalities, untranslatables and heterogeneities to evaporate in the production of universalistic 'objective' knowledge (see also Mowitt 1992; Bowman 2007). This is why, as Robert J. C. Young has argued, *anyone* can do postcolonial studies (Young 2003). One simply has to start from below. This 'below' always involves – as thinkers from Edward Said to Stuart Hall have asserted – something messy, dirty and mucky. This 'below', then, evokes both class and sexuality – and *therefore* ethnicity and gender.[3] It must, as Stuart Hall once put it, work on two fronts at the same time, saying yes and no at the same time (Hall 1992: 285). That is to say, as Hall has always argued, just as the critical and political impetus and genealogy of cultural studies as a simultaneously interdisciplinary and antidisciplinary 'self-reflexive' field (i.e., self-consciously theoretical and performative), it is also constitutively wedded to critical and political issues cortical to postcolonialism (i.e., those of language, power, culture, class, gender and ethnicity). So if it is of anything that 'I am' or this writing is the offspring, it is this disciplinary chiasmus – or, rather, this unrepentant undisciplined *mess*. Settling the genealogy of such a tangle has no proper place. Knowingly inhabiting this tangle in a particular way is vital. It is by exploring what I mean by this assertion that I would like to conclude.

Conclusion: The Tangled Web

The relationships between culture and the media are always complex, often unpredictable, and difficult to map out or chart with any certainty. Even one of the key pioneers of media and cultural studies, Stuart Hall – in other words, even one of the very people we might most expect to be able to make pronouncements about media and culture with some confidence and conviction – has argued that

> it has always been impossible in the theoretical field of cultural studies – whether it is conceived of in terms of texts and contexts, of intertextuality, or of the historical formations in which cultural practices are lodged – to get anything like an adequate theoretical account of culture's relations and its effects.
>
> (Hall 1992: 286)

Put differently, what Hall is saying here is no matter which way one approaches it, the complexity of culture and of the relations between culture and other realms, factors and forces (such as the economy – if that's not cultural – the state – if that's not cultural – or society and politics – if these are not cultural) always defies complete comprehension, complete codification, complete mapping or mastery. Culture is a tangled web of forces, interplays, contestations and conjunctures. This is why Hall always advocated the need for a 'conjunctural analysis' of historical contexts rather than simplistic (or complicated) attempts to understand things in isolation.

Hall was confident that conjunctural analysis would always be possible and could always help us to understand what is going on in the relations between forces, powers, agents and agencies. In this little book we have dipped our toes into the waters of a few places where media and culture seem to meet, always accompanied by other things, most notably politics or a political charge. And if nothing else, the sense of the political dimension to both media and culture, and the various sites of their complex interplay, is what I hope that this book has impressed upon you.

Culture and the media are part of ongoing tangled processes. They can work to stabilise or to destabilise states of affairs. They can reflect change or they may even precipitate change. They are sites and scenes of convention that can also be sites and scenes of the unconventional. Speaking of his approach to politics, philosophy and ethics, Jacques Derrida once put it like this:

> All that a deconstructive point of view tries to show is that since convention, institutions and consensus are stabilizations (sometimes stabilizations of great duration, sometimes micro-stabilizations), this means that they are stabilizations of something essentially unstable and chaotic. Thus it becomes necessary to stabilize precisely because stability is not natural; it is because there is instability that stabilization becomes necessary; it is because there is chaos that there is a need for stability. Now, this chaos and instability, which is fundamental, founding and irreducible, is at once naturally the worst against which we struggle with laws, rules, conventions, politics and provisional hegemony, but at the same time it is a chance, a chance to change, to destabilize. If there were continual stability, there would be no need for politics, and it is to the extent that stability is not natural, essential or substantial, that politics exists and ethics is possible. Chaos is at once a risk and a chance, and it is here that the possible and the impossible cross each other.
>
> (Derrida 1996: 84)

We can supplement Derrida's argument here by an understanding of the crucial importance that culture and the media play in constructing and disseminating ideas, representations and commonsense. Hence, culture and the media can play important roles in politics – sometimes progressively, sometimes regressively and sometimes unclearly. Culture and the media often work to close down change. But sometimes they help to open things up, revealing the biases, the censorships, the prejudices and injustices of culture and society. So they can often work to 'depoliticise'. But they always also have the potential to politicise and to be forces of change.

No one realm of culture or the media has a monopoly on importance. As we have started to explore in this book, film, TV, literature, pop music and other forms of writing, composition, construction and performance can all have influence and sway in any given situation. And what should be clear is that the 'consumption' of media and culture is often far from passive. Yet 'consuming media' is still often regarded as passive. As Jacques Rancière notes, for instance:

> according to the accusers, being a spectator is a bad thing for two reasons. First, viewing is the opposite of knowing: the spectator is held before an appearance in a state of ignorance about the process of production of this appearance and about the reality it conceals. Second, it is the opposite of acting: the spectator remains immobile in her seat, passive. To be a spectator is to be separated from both the capacity to know and the power to act.
>
> (Rancière 2009: 2)

But, he asks, 'what makes it possible to pronounce the spectator seated in her place inactive...? Why identify gaze and passivity...? Why assimilate listening to passivity, unless through the prejudice that speech is the opposite of action?' (Rancière 2009: 12). But, as we have seen throughout this book, viewing is not passive, looking is never neutral, listening is consequential, and speech is certainly not the opposite of action. Indeed, Rancière asserts

> Emancipation begins when we challenge the opposition between viewing and acting; when we understand that the self-evident facts that structure the relations between saying, seeing and doing themselves belong to the structure of domination and subjection. It begins when we understand that viewing is also an action that confirms or transforms this distribution of positions. The spectator also acts, like the pupil or scholar. She observes, selects, compares, interprets. She links what she sees to a host of other things that she has seen on other stages, in other kinds of place. She composes her own poem with the elements of the poem before her. She participates in the performance by refashioning it in her own way – by drawing back, for example, from the vital energy that it is supposed to transmit in order to make it a pure image and associate this image with a story which she has read or dreamt, experienced or invented. They are thus both distant spectators and active interpreters of the spectacle offered to them.
>
> (Rancière 2009: 13)

Notes

1 Culture Is (Not) the Media

1. The full passage is as follows: 'What is "familiarly known" is not properly known, just for the reason that it is "familiar". When engaged in the process of knowing, it is the commonest form of self-deception, and a deception of other people as well, to assume something to be familiar, and give assent to it on that very account. Knowledge of that sort, with all its talk, never gets from the spot, but has no idea that this is the case. Subject and object, and so on, God, nature, understanding, sensibility, etc., are uncritically presupposed as familiar and something valid, and become fixed points from which to start and to which to return. The process of knowing flits between these secure points, and in consequence goes on merely along the surface. Apprehending and proving consist similarly in seeing whether every one finds what is said corresponding to his idea too, whether it is familiar and seems to him so and so or not.' G. W. F. Hegel, *Phenomenology of Mind, Vol. I*, trans. J. B. Baillie (New York: Cosimo, 1910/2005), p. 92.
2. Given this connection between cultural scandal and sales, perhaps we also need to include 'marketing' or 'advertising' in our list of realms that are supposedly separate from 'culture' but that nevertheless have effects on or in 'it'.
3. 'In any case, literature is the right in principle to say anything, and it is to the great advantage of literature that is an operation at once political, democratic and *philosophical*, to the extent that literature allows one to pose questions that are often repressed in a philosophical context.' Jacques Derrida, 'Remarks on Deconstruction and Pragmatism', Chantal Mouffe (ed.) *Deconstruction and Pragmatism* (London: Routledge, 1996), p. 80.
4. 'The development of the word *culture* is a record of a number of important and continuing reactions to these changes in our social, economic and political life, and may be seen, in itself, as a special kind of map by means of which the nature of the changes can be explored.' Raymond Williams, *Culture and Society, 1780–1950* (New York: Columbia University Press, 1958), p. 16.

3 Media Representation and Its Cultural Consequences

1. Browne was hounded out of the oil industry because of homophobia. This all arose largely because of a court-case that Lord Brown initiated to try to prevent

the public revelation of his homosexuality. In it he committed perjury. He maintained a lie about another person's character for several weeks. However, he escaped punishment for this because the judge deemed public knowledge about his conduct to constitute punishment enough. A concise account of all of this can again be found on Wikipedia: http://en.wikipedia.org/wiki/John_Browne,_Baron_Browne_of_Madingley.

2. But more precisely, and what has been happening since May 2010 under the UK's coalition government, can be explained in terms provided by Naomi Klein. Klein writes in her book, *The Shock Doctrine* (see Naomi Klein's website: http://www.naomiklein.org/shock-doctrine) that, in response to disasters, it has become the unpublicised policy of neoliberal nation-states and their ministers and institutions, specifically the World Bank and the IMF, to offer 'help', to offer solutions; but solutions that are in fact slaves' ransoms: solutions which remake the world in their image, or rather, the image of economic organisation that they condone and seek impose everywhere. (See also Paul Kingsnorth on this: http://www.paulkingsnorth.net/onmy.html.)

3. See Robert J. C. Young: 'Even according to the rigorous analysis of Adam Smith's economics, then, in which education is constituted solely according to market forces, knowledge outside the orbit of a strict criterion of utility has to be invoked in order to provide something beyond the system that can save it from its own consequences. That philosophical knowledge can only not be assigned to the university because, having in the first instance been rigorously excluded, its introduction would contradict the rest of Smith's argument so absolutely as to call his entire premises into doubt' (Young 1992: 120–121).

4. See Robert J. C. Young: 'Smith discusses education in *Book 5* of *The Wealth of Nations* . . . Education falls under the category of a noneconomic institution whose ultimate benefit however makes it "in the highest degree advantageous to a great society." Smith then immediately focuses on the difference between what might be called the immediate and deferred profits of education: education is an institution whose use-value cannot be measured by the immediate exchange of its product, or, to put it another way, whose cost is greater than the direct exchange-value of the product that it produces, that is, the newly graduated student' (Young 1992: 114).

5. http://www.independent.co.uk/news/uk/politics/coalition-ready-for-strikes-as-pm-outlines-public-sector-revolution-2221701.html

4 Filming Culture

1. I use the 'ph' spelling here to highlight the psychoanalytic/cultural theoretical specificity of this usage. The 'ph' spelling is more likely to be used in British-English rather than American-English academic contexts in any case. However, elsewhere I use the 'f' spelling, usually where the 'ph' spelling would appear awkward, but also where psychoanalytic specificity is not necessary.

2. For Chow's elaboration of this notion of information target fields, see her *The Age of The World Target* (Chow 2006).
3. As Rey Chow clarifies: 'Race and ethnicity are...coterminous with sexuality, just as sexuality is implicated in race and ethnicity. [So], any analytical effort to keep these categories apart from one another may turn out to be counterproductive, for it is their categorical enmeshment – their categorical miscegenation, so to speak – that needs to be foregrounded' (Chow 2002: 7).

References

Adorno, Theodor W. and Max Horkheimer (1986), *Dialectic of Enlightenment*, London, Verso.

Arnold, Matthew (2009), *Culture and Anarchy*, Oxford, Oxford University Press.

Baudrillard, Jean (1994), *Simulacra and Simulation*, Ann Arbor, MI, University of Michigan Press.

BBC (2010), 'Police on Horseback Charge at Protestors (9th December)'. From http://www.bbc.co.uk/news/uk-11962905 (accessed 14 July 2012).

Blip.TV (2010), 'Police Officer U1202 Punches Student in Head'. From http://blip.tv/visionontv/police-officer-u1202-punches-student-in-head-4475870 (accessed 14 July 2012).

Bowman, Paul (2007), *Post-Marxism versus Cultural Studies: Theory, Politics and Intervention*, Edinburgh, Edinburgh University Press.

Bowman, Paul (2010), *Theorizing Bruce Lee: Film-Fantasy-Fighting-Philosophy*, Amsterdam and New York, Rodopi.

Chow, Rey (1991), *Woman and Chinese Modernity*, Minneapolis, MN and London, University of Minnesota Press.

Chow, Rey (1993), *Writing Diaspora: Tactics of Intervention in Contemporary Cultural Studies*, Bloomington, IN, Indiana University Press.

Chow, Rey (1995), *Primitive Passions: Visuality, Sexuality, Ethnography, and Contemporary Chinese Cinema*, New York, Columbia University Press.

Chow, Rey (1998), *Ethics after Idealism*, Bloomington, IN, Indiana University Press.

Chow, Rey (2002), *The Protestant Ethnic and the Spirit of Capitalism*, New York, Columbia University Press.

Chow, Rey (2006), *The Age of the World Target*, Durham and London, Duke.

Dale, Gareth (2010), 'Changing Interests: The Narrow Make-Up of the Browne Panel Provides Evidence of a Profound Shift in Higher Education Policymaking, Says Gareth Dale'. From http://www.timeshighereducation.co.uk/story.asp?sectioncode=26&storycode=414320&c=1 (accessed 14 July 2012).

Debord, Guy (1990), *Comments on the Society of the Spectacle*, London, Verso.

Debord, Guy (1994), *The Society of the Spectacle*, New York, Zone Books.

Derrida, Jacques (1981), *Dissemination*, London, Athlone.

Derrida, Jacques (1987), *The Post Card: From Socrates to Freud and Beyond*, Chicago and London, University of Chicago Press.

Derrida, Jacques (1996), 'Remarks on Deconstruction and Pragmatism'. *Deconstruction and Pragmatism*, ed. C. Mouffe. London, Routledge, 77–88.

Eliot, T. S. (1934), *After Strange Gods: A Primer of Modern Heresy, the Page-Barbour Lectures at the University of Virginia, 1933*, London, Faber and Faber.

Eliot, T. S. (1939), *The Idea of a Christian Society*, London, Faber.

Eliot, T. S. (1948), *Notes Towards the Definition of Culture*, London, Faber.

Foucault, Michel (1977), *Discipline and Punish: The Birth of the Prison*, New York, Pantheon Books.

Foucault, Michel (1978), *The History of Sexuality, Volume 1*, London, Penguin.

Foucault, Michel (1980), *Power/Knowledge: Selected Interviews and Other Writing, 1972–1977*, New York, Pantheon Books.

Guardian, The (2010), 'Student Protests: Video Shows Mounted Police Charging London Crowd'. From http://www.guardian.co.uk/uk/2010/nov/26/police-student-protests-horses-charge (accessed 14 July 2012).

Hall, Stuart (1992), 'Cultural Studies and Its Theoretical Legacies'. *Cultural Studies*, eds. Lawrence Grossberg, Cary Nelson and Paula Treichler. New York and London, Routledge, pp. 277–294.

Hall, Stuart (1994), 'Notes on Deconstructing "the Popular"'. *Cultural Theory and Popular Culture: A Reader*, ed. J. Storey. London, Harvester Wheatsheaf, 64–71.

Hegel, G. W. F. (1910, 2005), *Phenomenology of Mind*, New York, Cosimo.

Leavis, F. R. (1943), *Education & The University: A Sketch for an 'English School'*, London, Chatto & Windus.

Leavis, F. R. and Denys Thompson (1933), *Culture and Environment: The Training of Critical Awareness*, London, Chatto & Windus.

Lenin (2010), 'I am the mob', *Lenin's Tomb*.

Lyotard, Jean-François (1984), *The Postmodern Condition: A Report on Knowledge*, Minneapolis, MN, University of Minnesota Press.

Marx, Karl and Friedrich Engels (1967), *The Communist Manifesto*, Harmondsworth, Penguin.

McQuillan, Martin (2010a), 'The English Intifada and the Humanities' Last Stand'. From http://www.thelondongraduateschool.co.uk/thoughtpiece/the-english-intifada-and-the-humanities-last-stand/ (accessed 14 July 2012).

McQuillan, Martin (2010b), 'If You Tolerate This…: Lord Browne and the Privatisation of the Humanities'. From http://www.thelondongraduateschool.co.uk/thoughtpiece/if-you-tolerate-this%E2%80%A6-lord-browne-and-the-privatisation-of-the-humanities/ (accessed 14 July 2012).

Mowitt, John (1992), *Text: The Genealogy of an Antidisciplinary Object*, Durham and London, Duke.

Mulvey, Laura (1975), 'Visual Pleasure and Narrative Cinema', *Screen* 16(3): 6–18.

Park, Jane Chi Hyun (2010), *Yellow Future: Oriental Style in Hollywood Cinema*, Minneapolis, MN, University of Minnesota Press.

Peters, Micheal A. (2001), *Poststructuralism, Marxism and Neoliberalism: Between Theory and Politics*, London, Rowman and Littlefield.

Rancière, Jacques (1999), *Disagreement: Politics and Philosophy*, Minneapolis, MN, University of Minnesota Press.

Rancière, Jacques (2009), *The Emancipated Spectator*, London, Verso.

Red, Penny (2011), 'Panic on the Streets of London', *Penny Red*.

Said, Edward W. (1995), *Orientalism: Western Conceptions of the Orient*, London, Penguin.

Shaviro, Steven (2010), *Post-Cinematic Affect*, Winchester and Washington, DC, Zero Books.

Williams, Raymond (1958), *Culture and Society, 1780–1950*, New York, Columbia University Press.

Williams, Raymond (1976), *Keywords: A Vocabulary of Culture and Society*, London, Croom Helm.

Young, Robert J. C. (1992), 'The Idea of a Chrestomathic University'. *Logomachia: The Conflict of the Faculties*, ed. R. Rand. Lincoln and London, University of Nebraska Press, 99–122.

Young, Robert J. C. (2003), *Postcolonialism: A Very Short Introduction*, Oxford, Oxford University Press.

YouTube (2010), 'Students Protect Police Van'. From http://www.youtube.com/watch?v=gZoxzwlDeC8 (accessed 14 July 2012).

Žižek, Slavoj (2001), *On Belief*, London, Routledge.

Discography

Fifty Cent ft. Justin Timberlake (2007), 'Ayo Technology', Aftermath, Interscope, Shady.

Offspring, The (1998), 'Pretty Fly for a White Guy', Dexter Holland, Columbia Records.

Rage against the Machine (1992), 'Bullet in the Head', Garth Richardson.

Sex Pistols, The (1976), 'Anarchy in the UK', EMI.

Sex Pistols, The (1977), 'God Save the Queen', Virgin, A&M.

Filmography

American Gladiators (1989–97), Four Point Entertainment, Trans World International, USA.

American Psycho (2000), Mary Harron, USA.

Blade Runner (1982), Ridley Scott, USA.

Bourne Identity, The (2002), Doug Liman, USA.

Bourne Supremacy, The (2004), Paul Greengrass, USA.

Bourne Ultimatum, The (2007), Paul Greengrass, USA.

Fight Club (1999), David Fincher, USA.

Fist of Fury (1972), Lo Wei, HK.

High Fidelity (2000), Stephen Frears, UK.

Karate Kid, The (1984), John G. Avildsen, USA.

Kung Fu (1972–75), Ed Spielman, Jerry Thorpe, Herman Miller, USA.

Matrix, The (1999), Larry and Andy Wachowski, USA.
Minority Report (2002), Steven Speilberg, USA.
Muppet Show, The (1976–81), Jim Henson, USA.
Old Boy (2003), Chan-wook Park, Korea.
Pretty Woman (1990), Gary Marshall, USA.
Rambo (1985), George P. Cosmatos, USA
S1m0ne (2002), Andrew Nichol, USA.
Star Wars (1977), George Lucas, USA.
Street Fighter, The (1974), Shigehiro Ozawa, Japan.

Author Index